The World of
Marcel Duchamp

TIME LIFE BOOKS®

Other Publications

PLANET EARTH

LIBRARY OF HEALTH

CLASSICS OF THE OLD WEST

THE EPIC OF FLIGHT

THE GOOD COOK

THE SEAFARERS

THE ENCYCLOPEDIA OF COLLECTIBLES

THE GREAT CITIES

WORLD WAR II

HOME REPAIR AND IMPROVEMENT

THE WORLD'S WILD PLACES

THE TIME-LIFE LIBRARY OF BOATING

HUMAN BEHAVIOR

THE ART OF SEWING

THE OLD WEST

THE EMERGENCE OF MAN

THE AMERICAN WILDERNESS

THE TIME-LIFE ENCYCLOPEDIA OF GARDENING

LIFE LIBRARY OF PHOTOGRAPHY

THIS FABULOUS CENTURY

FOODS OF THE WORLD

TIME-LIFE LIBRARY OF AMERICA

GREAT AGES OF MAN

LIFE SCIENCE LIBRARY

THE LIFE HISTORY OF THE UNITED STATES

TIME READING PROGRAM

LIFE NATURE LIBRARY

LIFE WORLD LIBRARY

FAMILY LIBRARY

   HOW THINGS WORK IN YOUR HOME

   THE TIME-LIFE BOOK OF THE FAMILY CAR

   THE TIME-LIFE FAMILY LEGAL GUIDE

   THE TIME-LIFE BOOK OF FAMILY FINANCE

This volume is one of a series that surveys Western painting and sculpture from the end of the Middle Ages to the present.

 TIME-LIFE LIBRARY OF ART

The World of Marcel Duchamp

1887-1968

by Calvin Tomkins
and
the Editors of TIME-LIFE BOOKS

TIME-LIFE BOOKS, Alexandria, Virginia

Time-Life Books Inc.
is a wholly owned subsidiary of
TIME INCORPORATED

FOUNDER: Henry R. Luce 1898-1967

Editor-in-Chief: Henry Anatole Grunwald
President: J. Richard Munro
Chairman of the Board: Ralph P. Davidson
Executive Vice President: Clifford J. Grum
Chairman, Executive Committee: James R. Shepley
Editorial Director: Ralph Graves
Group Vice President, Books: Joan D. Manley
Vice Chairman: Arthur Temple

TIME-LIFE BOOKS INC.
MANAGING EDITOR: Jerry Korn
Text Director: George Constable
Board of Editors: Dale M. Brown, George G. Daniels,
Thomas H. Flaherty Jr., Martin Mann, Philip W.
Payne, Gerry Schremp, Gerald Simons
Planning Director: Edward Brash
Art Director: Tom Suzuki
    Assistant: Arnold C. Holeywell
Director of Administration: David L. Harrison
Director of Operations: Gennaro C. Esposito
Director of Research: Carolyn L. Sackett
    Assistant: Phyllis K. Wise
Director of Photography: Dolores A. Littles

CHAIRMAN: John D. McSweeney
President: Carl G. Jaeger
Executive Vice Presidents: John Steven Maxwell,
David J. Walsh
Vice Presidents: George Artandi, Stephen L. Bair,
Peter G. Barnes, Nicholas Benton, John L. Canova,
Beatrice T. Dobie, Carol Flaumenhaft, James L.
Mercer, Herbert Sorkin, Paul R. Stewart

TIME-LIFE LIBRARY OF ART
SERIES EDITOR: Robert Morton
Editorial Staff for *The World of Marcel Duchamp:*
Editor: Percy Knauth
Designer: Paul Jensen
Assistant Designer: Leonard Wolfe
Staff Writer: Tim Carr
Chief Researcher: Martha T. Goolrick
Researchers: Yvonne Chan, Adrian Condon,
Judith Levenson, Susan Marcus, Iris Unger
Copy Coordinator: Muriel Clarke
Picture Coordinator: Patricia Maye
Art Assistant: Nanci Earle

EDITORIAL OPERATIONS
Production Director: Feliciano Madrid
    Assistants: Peter A. Inchauteguiz,
    Karen A. Meyerson
Copy Processing: Gordon E. Buck
Quality Control Director: Robert L. Young
    Assistant: James J. Cox
    Associates: Daniel J. McSweeney, Michael G. Wight
Art Coordinator: Anne B. Landry
Copy Room Director: Susan B. Galloway
    Assistants: Celia Beattie, Ricki Tarlow

For information about any Time-Life book,
please write:
Reader Information
Time-Life Books
541 North Fairbanks Court
Chicago, Illinois 60611

About the Author

Calvin Tomkins met and became friendly with Marcel Duchamp while doing a profile of the artist for *The New Yorker* magazine, where Mr. Tomkins is a staff writer. He is the author of *The Bride and the Bachelors*, a collection of profiles that includes, besides Duchamp, the painter Robert Rauschenberg, the sculptor Jean Tinguely and the composer John Cage. A former writer for Radio Free Europe and a General Editor at *Newsweek* magazine, Mr. Tomkins is the author of *Off the Wall: The Art World of Our Time.*

The Consulting Editor

H. W. Janson is Professor of Fine Arts at New York University. Among his numerous books and publications are his definitive *History of Art, The Sculpture of Donatello* and *The Story of Painting for Young People,* which he co-authored with his wife.

The Consultant for This Book

George Heard Hamilton has rendered invaluable assistance in the preparation of this book, having read the text in its entirety and given expert advice on the preparation of the picture essays. Presently Professor of Art at Williams College and Director Emeritus of the Sterling and Francine Clark Art Institute, Williamstown, Mass., Professor Hamilton is both teacher and author. His books include *Manet and His Critics* and *Art and Architecture of Russia* and translations of works both by and about his friend Marcel Duchamp.

On the Slipcase

Roue de Bicyclette, an early Duchamp readymade, is a bicycle wheel placed upside down on a stool. This is the third version of the 1913 original.

End Papers

Marcel Duchamp is seen through the glass of his *The Bride Stripped Bare by Her Bachelors, Even* at the Philadelphia Museum of Art.

CORRESPONDENTS: Elisabeth Kraemer (Bonn); Margot Hapgood, Dorothy Bacon (London); Susan Jonas, Lucy T. Voulgaris (New York); Maria Vincenza Aloisi, Josephine du Brusle (Paris); Ann Natanson (Rome). Valuable assistance was also provided by: Friso Endt (Amsterdam); George Taber (Brussels); Barbara Moir (London); Piero Saporiti (Madrid); Carolyn T. Chubet (New York); Joan Dupont (Paris); Erik Amfitheatrof (Rome); Mary Johnson (Stockholm).

Library of Congress Cataloguing in Publication Data
Tomkins, Calvin, 1925-
    The world of Marcel Duchamp, 1887-   by Calvin Tomkins
    and the editors of Time-Life Books. New York, Time, Inc.
    [1966] 192 p. illus. (part col.) ports. (part col.) 31 cm.
    (Time-Life library of art)
    Bibliography: p. 185.
    1. Duchamp, Marcel, 1887-   I. Time-Life Books.
    II. Title.
    N6853.D8T6   709.04   66-28544
ISBN 0-8094-0207-6
ISBN 0-8094-0265-3 lib. bdg.
ISBN 0-8094-0236-X ret. ed.

Contents

I

A Most Unlikely
Patron Saint

The world has changed less since Jesus Christ than it has in the last thirty years.—CHARLES PEGUY, 1913.

The discovery that Marcel Duchamp was one of the most influential artists of the 20th Century has been a recent development in modern art history. Not many critics would have assigned him such a leading role before 1950, and some of our esthetic guardians are outraged by the immense reputation given to him in recent years. Like everything else about Duchamp, this reputation is firmly rooted in paradox.

What are we to make of a painter who, having begun his painting career in 1902, abandoned it for good in 1923—preferring, as legend has it, to spend his time playing chess? Was Duchamp playing a consummately clever game all those years, as one hostile critic has suggested —waging a quietly diabolical "anti-art" campaign in order to cover up what was in effect his own failure as an artist? Or is it true, as his many admirers insist, that he never lifted a finger to advance his own reputation and that he was indifferent to fame? What does being anti-art mean, anyway? And if Duchamp really was anti-art, how did he manage to serve as inspiration and guide to so many artists, from the Dadaists and Surrealists of the 1920s and 1930s to the current crop of young American painters—for whom Duchamp, an occasional New York resident from 1915 until his death and a United States citizen after 1955, became a sort of patron saint, a legendary figure? The answers to some of these questions should suggest themselves here, but it must be clearly stated at the outset that there is no single explanation to the enigma of Marcel Duchamp. It will be seen, moreover, that the questions raised by his long and unusual career lead straight to the sources of modern art, over whose development his unique and complex intelligence presided, somewhat ironically, for half a century.

Looking back over that eventful epoch to the seed time of the modern movement, what strikes one first is the extraordinary ability of some artists to prophesy the future. This ability was never more clearly demonstrated than in the years immediately preceding the First World War. The political upheavals, the breakup of traditional ideals and beliefs, the spiritual unease and social chaos that followed this cataclysm could all be detected in the fantastically proliferating art movements of the

Long ignored by the art public and appreciated by few of his contemporaries, Duchamp—seen here at a 1961 show in New York—is being increasingly valued as the most potent influence on the diverse, antitraditional arts of the mid-20th Century.

prewar period. Nor were the visual artists the only ones to feel the imminence of great change. Poets and novelists also sensed the coming destruction of the old order, and many of the period's greatest names—James Joyce and André Gide, Gertrude Stein and Guillaume Apollinaire—were those who forged the new tools with which to create an entirely new kind of literature. In music, the harsh dissonances of Stravinsky's *Sacre du Printemps* goaded the audience attending its 1913 premiere to riot; at about the same time, the Viennese Arnold Schönberg had arrived at the 12-tone technique that would soon challenge the conventional harmonic scale. The avant-garde painters and sculptors were ahead of their literary and musical colleagues, though, in their decisive break with the past. With courage born of despair, they responded to the disintegration of their society by rejecting most of the traditional concepts on which Western art had been based since classical times and creating a new basis and a new function for art itself.

Although the origins of this revolutionary attitude can be found in certain aspects of Impressionism and Post-Impressionism, and above all in the work of Paul Cézanne, the real breakthrough occurred during those years leading up to 1914, and the man mainly responsible for it was Pablo Picasso. Having shattered the visual form of familiar objects to create the new structure called Cubism, Picasso proceeded, together with his great ally, Georges Braque, to take an enormously important further step; the two began, in 1911, to use the fragmented forms of natural objects as free elements in new visual structures whose relation to the original objects was often not readily apparent—structures whose primary basis lay in the artist's own imagination. Meanwhile a number of other artists in different places—Wassily Kandinsky in Munich, Robert Delaunay and Frank Kupka in Paris, Arthur Dove in America—also began to free themselves more and more from the representation of specific objects in any form, and to move toward a totally abstract art. It was what the critic Herbert Read has called the "moment of liberation" for Western art—the watershed between an art that had always been, in one way or another, an interpretation of the visual world, and an art that existed independently on the canvas as a new object, a pure fruit of the imagination.

Duchamp's early maturity as a painter coincided with this historic moment. Six years younger than Picasso, he made only a minor contribution to Cubism—although his Cubist *Nude Descending a Staircase* was the sensation of the 1913 Armory Show in New York. It was in his response to the new concept of art as an imaginative adventure that Duchamp showed his profound originality. While many of the leading Cubists like Albert Gleizes, Jean Metzinger and others labored to turn the Cubist revolution into a new orthodoxy, Duchamp kept right on asking the same troublesome questions about the nature of art and the nature of reality that had led to the revolution in the first place. He even went so far as to question the visual basis of painting. Why should art be limited to purely visual architecture, now that the artist was freed of his old dependence on the exterior world? "I wanted to get away from the physical aspect of painting," Duchamp said in 1946. "I was interested in ideas—not merely in visual products. I wanted to put painting once again at the service of the mind."

Duchamp believed that in spite of the sweeping revolution that already had taken place art was still being thought of as a purely "retinal" affair—something whose appeal was directed solely or primarily to the eye. Up until the time of Gustave Courbet, he maintained, all European painting had been either literary or religious; it was Courbet who in the mid-19th Century introduced the retinal emphasis, or what Duchamp in another connection has called the "olfactory" art of painters who are in love with the smell of paint and who have no interest in re-creating ideas on canvas. This retinal bias had been accepted by the Impressionists and subsequent schools, reaching its apogee in the art of Picasso and Henri Matisse, who, despite their profoundly original contributions, were still "retinals" at heart. It also led to the glorification of the manual side of painting, the craft aspect, and it was against this that Duchamp rebelled. "All through the last half of the 19th Century in France there was an expression, '*bête comme un peintre*' [as stupid as a painter]," Duchamp said. "And it was true—that kind of painter who just puts down what he sees *is* stupid. In my case I was thinking a little too much, maybe, but I don't care, that's what I thought."

In his aristocratic refusal to be a mere retinal painter or to limit himself to the craft of painting alone, Duchamp has occasionally been compared to that most mysterious of geniuses, Leonardo da Vinci. Both men were dedicated in a sense to the limitless concept of art as idea, art as a mental act, and both considered painting merely one among many possible activities of the mind. Unlike Leonardo, though, Duchamp never really moved outside the sphere of art, and all his inventions and experiments, even those most often castigated as being "anti-art," have served as stepping stones for his followers. The "readymades," for example—those utilitarian objects such as hat racks and snow shovels that Duchamp promoted to the status of "works of art" by the mere act of signing them—the readymades have had their echoes in the *objets trouvés* (found objects) of the Surrealists and the junk sculpture of a later generation; furthermore, the highly disturbing questions that the readymades raised with regard to the nature of art and the function of the artist are now being asked in much the same fashion by a whole group of young artists to whom the label "Pop" is rather loosely applied. Duchamp's early experiments with objects in motion—rotary machines, revolving disks, abstract cinema—foreshadowed the current fascination with kinetic sculpture and film making. His cover design for a 1936 issue of the magazine *Cahiers d'Art*, two superimposed hearts whose sharply contrasting colors set up a strong chromatic vibration, introduced an optical principle that was rediscovered 25 years later by the inventors of "Op" art, and his astonishing *mise-en-scène* for several international Surrealist exhibitions during the 1930s and 1940s presaged the spectator-involving "happenings" and "environments" of the 1950s and 1960s.

Duchamp never bothered to capitalize on his innovations; his interest lay solely in the principle, and the technical means by which to achieve it. "All this business of my being influential has been very much exaggerated," he said once, "but what little there is in it is probably due to my Cartesian mind. I refused to accept anything on faith. So, doubting everything, I had to find in my work something that had not existed before. And then, of course, once having done something, I didn't want to repeat it."

Although it may sometimes appear that everything Duchamp ever said or did has been mined for esthetic significance by later artists, collectors, dealers and critics, not very many of his admirers have shared his skepticism regarding the ultimate value of art. Beginning his career at a time when the artist was an outsider, scorned by and contemptuous of the commercial middle class, he witnessed the triumphant penetration of the middle class by these same artists, usually on their own terms. Bourgeois society ended by accepting art as one more commodity and status symbol, and it embraced the artist as a new cultural demigod, on a par with the film star and the television personality.

All this left Duchamp feeling somewhat dubious. The commercialization of art, which he saw beginning right after the First World War, almost certainly influenced his own withdrawal from painting in 1923. The tendency of so many of his fellow artists, once they had gained standing among the bourgeois, to strike public attitudes and to lose their sense of humor—to become, as he once put it, "the last word in divinity"—struck him as ridiculous. Duchamp believed wholeheartedly in the need for humor, but he was not convinced of the need for art. "Art," he said, "is a habit-forming drug. That's all it is for the artist, for the collector, for anybody connected with it. Art has absolutely no existence as veracity, as truth. People speak of it with great, religious reverence, but I don't see why it is to be so much revered. I'm afraid I'm an agnostic when it comes to art. I don't believe in it with all the mystical trimmings. As a drug it's probably very useful for many people, very sedative, but as a religion it's not even as good as God."

Now that Duchamp's own work has entered into the pantheon of art history, where it shows every indication of taking out permanent membership, one might assume that he risked nothing by such an attitude. It should be remembered, however, that until fairly recently Duchamp's reputation was an underground one, that his public recognition as one of the masters of 20th Century art dates only from about 1954, and that he nevertheless acted on his iconoclastic beliefs all his life. He showed very clearly that what he valued most was not art but life itself, not the creation of masterpieces but the free play of the intelligence. This attitude, more than any single factor, underlies his extraordinary influence and his legendary status today. "Art is only one occupation among others," he once said. "It's not all my life, far from it." Among his latter-day admirers and disciples, there are many who believe that of all Duchamp's works of art his most original, without a doubt, was his own life.

In the remarkable family of artists sired by M. Eugène Duchamp, a well-to-do notary in the Rouen region of Normandy, questions of temperament or ambition were never allowed to dilute the warm affection that its members felt toward one another. Marcel, the third of six chil-

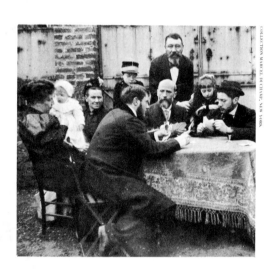

COLLECTION MARCEL DUCHAMP, NEW YORK

This photograph from a family album, made in the late 1890s, shows the Duchamp family relaxing in their garden. Identified are, from left to right, Madame Duchamp (with the baby on her lap), Marcel (wearing a military cap), Jacques (foreground), Monsieur Duchamp (seated, center), and Suzanne and Raymond. Following in their father's footsteps (he was a notary), the Duchamp sons began professional careers; but art eventually diverted them all.

dren, was born on July 28, 1887. He recalled his childhood as being quite normal and happy, and there was certainly no struggle involved in his decision to become an artist; his two older brothers, Gaston and Raymond, had both made that decision before him. Their father was so tolerant in this respect that when Gaston, Raymond, Marcel and finally their younger sister Suzanne left the roost one by one and went off to Paris to become artists, he agreed to provide each one with a small income to get started on. At the same time, with typical French practicality, he took careful note of the individual sums advanced and later deducted the total from each child's inheritance. This tolerance for art was supported by their mother, a talented amateur musician whose father, Emile-Frédéric Nicolle, had combined a business career as a Rouen shipping agent with an avocation as an engraver. His prints and paintings were prominently displayed on the walls of the comfortable family house in the village of Blainville, where Marcel grew up.

Like his older brothers, Duchamp showed a precocious talent for drawing and sketching. Most of his apprentice work has been lost, but what there is of it shows Duchamp rapidly assimilating the art of the recent past as he catches up with his own time. He was an Impressionist at 15, in the 1902 *Landscape at Blainville*, which is his earliest surviving oil *(page 17)*. By 1904, when he joined his brothers in Paris and entered the Académie Julian, his portraits and landscapes showed the unmistakable influence of Cézanne. After a year out for his compulsory military service, he returned to Paris toward the end of 1906 and started painting in the bold, discordant colors of the Fauve School, then at its peak under the leadership of Matisse. Duchamp continued to paint in the Fauve style until 1910—portraits for the most part, although the number of female nude studies shows his growing predilection for this subject. Like a good many artists then, including his brothers, he supported himself mainly by doing occasional illustrations for newspapers such as *Le Courrier Français* and *Le Rire*. His facility as a draftsman was obvious; in fact, one gains the impression from these occasional drawings that for Duchamp mere facility was something of a problem, a trap to be sedulously avoided. "Marcel never had any trouble painting," one contemporary artist has said of him. In 1910, though, he had not yet managed to catch up with the latest developments in art.

Among the first works of art young Marcel ever saw were etchings by his maternal grandfather Emile-Frédéric Nicolle, an engraver and painter. This one, showing the Cathedral of Notre Dame in Paris, is one of his finest. Both Jacques, who earned international fame as an engraver, and Marcel were skilled in the graphic processes.

The Cubist revolution, announced by Picasso's large 1907 canvas *Les Demoiselles d'Avignon*, had shaken European art to its roots. Far more drastically than any previous art movement, Cubism rejected all traditional esthetic notions and demanded a completely new way of looking not only at art but at the world. The Cubist painter jettisoned conventional beauty, the imitation of nature, the illusion of space through perspective; he deliberately broke up the form of things so that he might be free to paint his own vision of the inner reality—in Picasso's famous phrase, "not what you see, but what you know is there." Reactions to such a total upheaval of esthetic values were intense and violent, among artists as well as the general public.

At about the same time, the Futurist movement in Italy, which began in 1909, was fomenting a revolution of a different sort. Futurism began as a literary movement, spearheaded by the Italian poet and dramatist Filippo Tommaso Marinetti, and dedicated to throwing off the yoke of outworn traditions that had made Italy a mausoleum of antiquities and prevented Italians from paying much attention to new ideas in art. "Burn the museums!" "Destroy the libraries!" cried Futurist speakers at sensational public demonstrations throughout Italy.

The public replied with insults and overripe fruit, but Marinetti's intoxicating cry of modernism rang around the world. In essence, it was an exhortation to get out of the past and into the machine age. "We declare that the world's splendor has been enriched by a new beauty; the beauty of speed," Marinetti had said in the first Futurist manifesto, published in the Paris paper *Le Figaro* in 1909. "A racing motor car, its frame adorned with great pipes, like snakes with explosive breath . . . a roaring motor car, which looks as though running on shrapnel, is more beautiful than the *Victory of Samothrace*." A second manifesto in 1910, signed by the Italian painters Boccioni, Carrà, Russolo, Balla and Severini, extended Futurism to the visual arts. The ruling principle of Futurist art was dynamism. Instead of painting a "fixed moment," the Futurist painters sought to reproduce on canvas "the dynamic sensation" of life itself, and by this they meant the modern "life of steel, of pride, of fever and of speed."

Sometimes described as the first anti-art movement, Futurism also rebelled against "the tyranny of the terms 'harmony' and 'good taste.'" In a later manifesto, Boccioni proclaimed the need to "ABOLISH IN SCULPTURE as in every other art the TRADITIONAL SUBLIMITY OF THE SUBJECT," and called for the replacement of marble and bronze by such materials as "glass, wood, cardboard, iron, cement, horsehair, leather, cloth, mirrors, electric lights, etc., etc." Oddly enough, Picasso and Braque were actually using some of these "ignoble" materials in their own collages at the time. Cubism, however, maintained its formal esthetic basis, while Futurism did not. As the art historian Joshua C. Taylor puts it, the Futurists "substituted activity for form and excitement for contemplation." Their utter disdain for the traditional goals of high art had a profound influence on subsequent developments and prepared the way for the much more aggressively anti-art movement called Dadaism.

From 1910 on, the Cubists and the Futurists were engaged in a rivalry that became increasingly bitter. The Cubists claimed, with justification, that the Futurists had appropriated some of their plastic ideas and technical methods. The Futurists replied that the Cubists were chained to the past, and that they were creating an academism that was even more rigid than the one they had overthrown.

In this era of artistic revolutions and polemics, moreover, the Cubists did not always see eye to eye even with one another. Picasso and Braque represented the advance guard of Cubism. They worked together so closely from 1909 to 1914—"like mountaineers roped together," as Braque described it—that it was sometimes difficult for them to tell their own canvases apart. By 1912, they were beginning to introduce wood, sand, printed letters and other "unartistic" elements into paint-

Like many other French artists, including Daumier before him, young Duchamp made satirical drawings for popular magazines. The one above, titled *Femme-Cocher*, pokes fun at the introduction of women drivers and taxi meters on the horse-drawn cabs of Paris: in Duchamp's cartoon, neither of the innovations is working. Although he made little money from them, these cartoons may have fostered his lifelong delight in puns and anagrams and started his habit of captioning his works.

ings that no longer showed much trace of representation. A number of the Paris artists who had embraced Cubism hesitated to go this far; specifically, they were not yet willing to relinquish entirely the imitation of natural objects in some form. Most of these so-called "reasonable" Cubists met regularly in the Parisian suburb of Puteaux, where Duchamp's two brothers had their studio. In addition, the Puteaux group included the artists Fernand Léger, Gleizes, Metzinger, Roger de la Fresnaye, Henri le Fauconnier, André Lhote and Delaunay. They exhibited together in Paris at the annual Salon des Indépendants and the Salon d'Automne, and later formed a separate exhibiting group that they called the Salon de la Section d'Or, or Salon of the Golden Section. They remained at all times separate from Picasso and Braque, who exhibited mainly at the Galerie Kahnweiler and who tended, according to Duchamp, to look with disdain upon their "reasonable" followers.

Both of Duchamp's brothers had adopted new names when they arrived in Paris and embarked on their artistic careers. Gaston, the eldest, called himself Jacques Villon—a reference to the French medieval poet-outlaw François Villon that seems curious in relation to his own quiet, lifelong development as a marvelously subtle painter and printmaker. Raymond had compromised with Duchamp-Villon; considered by many of their contemporaries to be the most naturally gifted of the Duchamp brothers, he was then engaged in applying the principles of Cubism to the art of sculpture. Neither Marcel nor his sister Suzanne found it necessary to disguise their somewhat prosaic patronymic, although events would soon prove Marcel to be the most daring innovator of the family. Among the artists who met each Sunday at his brothers' studio in Puteaux, Marcel was at first accepted with a certain condescension as a promising fellow—talented, to be sure, but not exactly a threat. Duchamp found the Cubists singularly lacking in humor, at least where their art was concerned. He took no part in their endless discussions of Cubist theory, which bored him stiff, and gained a reputation for shyness as a result.

The only artist with whom Duchamp found much in common at this time was Francis Picabia, a brilliant and rather wild young man, eight years his senior, who had recently been converted to Cubism after winning a reputation as a painter in the Impressionist style. Picabia claimed to be descended from the old Spanish nobility and, thanks to the generosity of his father, a wealthy Cuban then serving as an attaché to the Cuban legation in Paris, he was able to live on a grand scale. He had a large income, which he spent lavishly, and a precocious talent —as a child, he had replaced the old masters in his father's house with copies of his own, and then sold the originals to get money for his stamp collection. Picabia's exuberant temperament found its release in fast cars, pretty women and an iconoclastic sense of humor that was the natural overflow of a flamboyant personality.

Duchamp's humor was more subtle and more difficult to account for. Asked once whether there had been much laughter in the notary's house in Blainville, Duchamp thought for a moment and replied, "No, not really. My mother was the saddest person—she was quite deaf,

Jacques Villon, shown above at his drawing board in a sketch by his brother Marcel, earned money as a young artist by doing illustrations for newspapers and magazines. Although his small success persuaded his father that he might make a career as an artist rather than as a lawyer, it was many years before Jacques could free himself from making prints of other artists' works to achieve the reputation his talent merited.

and it made her rather somber. My father had a tiny form of humor, and my brothers a little more. I don't know where it came from, really. I always hated the seriousness of life. By using humor, though, you can be excused from engaging in very serious considerations. It is an escape, I suppose."

Although Duchamp steered clear of the ultra-serious discussions of the Puteaux group, he did succeed in assimilating the lessons of Cubism. Toward the end of 1910, he had abandoned Fauvism and started to work in the muted colors and the flat, broken planes of the Cubist style. His 1911 canvas *Sonata (page 24),* a delicate Cubist rendering of a family concert by his mother and three sisters, was well received by the Puteaux artists, as was his *Portrait of Chess Players (page 23).* Other Duchamp paintings of that same year provide evidence, however, of his increasing preoccupation with ideas that went beyond Cubism. In *Portrait (page 25),* for example, the figure of a woman is repeated five times—Duchamp has said she was someone he saw on the street and never met, but loved on sight. The five images suggest the idea of movement through space, a pictorial idea that was of considerable interest to the Futurists but not to the Cubists, whose art was essentially static. Duchamp's infatuation with the lady is obscured by a touch of the emerging Duchampian irony: in three of the figures she is clothed, while in the two others she is naked. All the figures seem to spring from a single source at the painting's base, like flowers in a vase.

Duchamp's interest in mechanical forms and the representation of movement was expressed very early in this *Coffee Mill* painted as a decoration for his brother Raymond's kitchen. The sequential rotation of the grinder's handle foreshadows the stop-motion technique of *Nude Descending a Staircase;* the object itself anticipates the *Chocolate Grinder* Duchamp used in the *Large Glass* some years later.

In *Yvonne and Magdeleine Torn in Tatters,* the Cubist breaking-up and reconstruction of forms has been used to indicate a movement through time rather than space—overlapping profile views of his two youngest sisters show their progression from youth to old age *(page 24). Sad Young Man in a Train,* painted late in 1911, abandons representation altogether *(page 26).* Duchamp has said that the sad young man is himself, on the occasion of a train trip home to Rouen; the title is thus a piece of self-irony, Duchamp making fun of the self-conscious sorrows of youth. With this painting, whose interlocking planes suggest machinery in motion, Duchamp entered the world of strange, mechanical imagery that would absorb him for the rest of his painting career. His ability to invest machines with a fantastic life of their own shows up for the first time in a small painting he did later in 1911, *Coffee Mill,* which Duchamp has often said was the basis for much of his later work. Both the *Sad Young Man in a Train* and the *Coffee Mill,* moreover, led directly to the creation of a work that proved altogether too revolutionary for his fellow Cubists.

Like almost all the major paintings that Duchamp would do from then on, this one originated from a verbal, poetic source. In the fall of 1911, Duchamp made three sketches to illustrate a collection of poems by the Symbolist poet Jules Laforgue. The first drawing, called *Encore à Cet Astre,* which is now in the Arensberg Collection at the Philadelphia Museum of Art, shows a fairly recognizable nude figure climbing a flight of stairs *(page 15).* "That first study was almost naturalistic," Duchamp has said. "At least, it showed some hunks of flesh. Right after that, though, in January of 1912, I started in to make a big painting of the same subject that was a long way from being naturalistic. There were other changes, too. At first, in the sketch for Laforgue's poem, I had had the nude *ascending*, but then I began to think that it would help my expression to have her descending. More majestic, you know— the way it's done in the music halls, when the girls come down those long flights of stairs." Duchamp worked for a month on the painting, in which the nude figure emerged as a sort of mechanized abstraction in downward motion. He entitled it *Nu Descendant un Escalier (Nude Descending a Staircase)*—painting the title on the lower part of the canvas so that the words could function both visually and mentally as part of the composition *(page 27)*. In March he sent it to the Salon des Indépendants, where the Puteaux Cubists were mounting an exhibition.

The furor caused by Duchamp's large *Nude* indicates how seriously the Cubists took their theories in those days. Just a month before, in February 1912, the first major exhibition of Futurist paintings in Paris had opened at the Galerie Bernheim-Jeune. Duchamp himself did not see any Futurist work until he had finished his own painting, and he does not even recall having read the Futurist manifestoes. The actual composition of *Nude Descending a Staircase*, like that of the earlier *Sad Young Man in a Train*, had been suggested to him by Jules Etienne Marey's first chronophotographs of moving figures, which were appearing then in the illustrated magazines.

Futurism's shock tactics were headline news from Berlin to Tokyo, however, and there had been a great deal of argument in Paris about the Futurists' intention to express the "universal dynamism" of life through a "style of motion." To a number of the Cubists, notably the rather doctrinaire Gleizes and Metzinger, it looked very much as though Duchamp had sent in a picture that veered close to Futurism in its attempt to express motion through space. The painting not only smacked of Futurism to them but its subject seemed in addition to mock the Cubist theories. Cubism had limited its subject matter to a few simple, everyday objects—the café table, the carafe, the wineglass, the pipe, the guitar. A nude of any sort was not considered a proper subject for a Cubist (or for a Futurist either—the 1910 Futurist manifesto had denounced the nude in painting as "nauseous and tedious," and demanded its total suppression for 10 years). And as for a nude *descending*, and a mechanical nude at that. . . . Could Duchamp be making fun of everyone? Humor was not permissible in the revolutionary climate of early Cubism, when a united front had to be maintained against the hostile public. To deal with this unpleasant crisis, the Puteaux Cubists called a conference from which Duchamp was excluded. Shortly thereafter, Jacques Villon and Raymond Duchamp-Villon, soberly dressed for the occasion, paid a formal call on their younger brother and suggested that he withdraw his picture from the Indépendants show, or at the very least paint out the title and call it something else.

"I said nothing to my brothers," Duchamp recalled. "But I went immediately to the show and took my painting home in a taxi. It was really a turning point in my life, I can assure you. I saw that I would not be very much interested in groups after that."

Duchamp's illustration for a poem by Jules Laforgue, *Encore à Cet Astre (Once More to This Star)*, contains the germinal idea for his *Nude Descending a Staircase*—although the figure on the right here is climbing rather than descending. The sketch was made in 1911, a few months before the painting, but Duchamp did not sign it until 1912. After the Armory Show he countersigned it with a greeting to the art dealer who had bought *Nude*, sight unseen, by telegram, for $324.

Evolution of a Rebel

Painting has always bored me," said Marcel Duchamp in 1964, "except at the very beginning, when there was that feeling of opening the eyes to something new." In the beginning, as a boy in the 1890s, he was surrounded by art—and by artists. His brothers, the painter Jacques Villon and the sculptor Raymond Duchamp-Villon, were in the thick of an art world bursting with new ideas and energies. His childhood home was filled with seascapes, landscapes and etchings by his grandfather Emile-Frédéric Nicolle. "When you see so many paintings," said Duchamp, "you've got to paint." In 1904, at the age of 17, he resolved to become an artist.

He could not have chosen a more exciting time. Paris was reverberating from the first Cézanne retrospective show; Matisse was experimenting with the vivid colors that would soon give birth to Fauvism; a few years later, Picasso and Braque would create Cubism.

Duchamp dallied with each of the new styles, but no adopted mode could satisfy him. "A technique can be learned but you can't learn to have an original imagination," he later said. By the time he was 25, he found himself with nowhere to go except into unexplored territory. His extraordinary progress from his early Impressionist works to the machinelike paintings of his maturity reveals the originality of his inquiring and restless mind—and forecasts the profound influence he was to exercise on art and artists for decades to come.

At the age of 15, Duchamp, who was to become a leading renegade in his generation, painted this —his first oil—with the bright colors and relaxed brushwork of Impressionists such as Pissarro and Monet, who were pioneers in an earlier generation.

Landscape at Blainville, 1902

Bust Portrait of Chauvel, 1910

Suzanne Seated, 1902

Portrait of Magdeleine, 1905

Like most young artists, Duchamp began by painting the subjects closest to him—his family and friends. That he had a good grasp of conventional techniques can be seen in the captivating watercolor portraits of his sisters *(right)*. He received his only formal training at the Académie Julian in Paris, a sort of preparatory studio for the Ecole des Beaux-Arts. But he despised the academic atmosphere and dropped out after 18 months to pursue his own tastes.

When, at age 23, he painted the portrait of his father he had adopted Cézanne's planar color construction, a dynamic restructuring of landscapes and the human form that was to lead inexorably to Cubism. At about the same time, he was experimenting with Fauvism, the art of the "wild beasts." Like Matisse, the pioneer of that style, Duchamp had no qualms about adopting arbitrary colors, such as the blue hair, purple-splotched face and blood-red lips he gave his friend Chauvel *(above)*.

But many artists were seeking a more intellectual approach to painting. Cubism, with its carefully structured planes and its almost monochromatic palette, offered such a way.

Portrait of the Artist's Father, Seated, 1910

19

Jacques Villon: *Little Girl at the Piano,* 1912

Jean Metzinger: *Tea Time*, 1911

The Duchamp brothers in their garden at Puteaux, c. 1912

Juan Gris: *The Man in the Café*, 1912

By 1911 a dozen or more young Cubists, scorned by the public and art dealers alike, had joined forces and were meeting regularly at the studios of Duchamp's brothers at Puteaux. A year later they held their first exhibition, called the Salon of the Golden Section, after an ancient mathematical formula for ideal proportion that fascinated them.

The Puteaux Cubists, who were consciously rebelling against the casual or "intuitive" style practiced by Picasso and Braque, plotted their paintings with geometrical precision. However, Jacques Villon, who is considered the most lyrical painter in the group, concealed his draftsmanship beneath subtly blended areas of pure color.

Jean Metzinger, according to his friend and colleague Albert Gleizes, insisted "that all the parts of his work shall tally with each other logically and justify each other down to the smallest detail"—a statement borne out by his *Tea Time (left, above)*. Juan Gris was so obsessed with geometry that he plotted lines and rectangles on his canvas until a subject suggested itself; he then added color and a few appropriate finishing touches.

Duchamp, though he rarely joined in the debates, was a welcome member of the Puteaux group, and his paintings were well received—for the time being.

21

Duchamp

What Cubism meant to Duchamp is immediately evident from these two paintings. Scarcely a year separates them, and they deal with the same theme—a chess match between Duchamp's brothers—yet in technique the two have nothing in common. What had been merely a pleasant afternoon's recreation in the earlier painting has been transformed, in the Cubist version, into a vigorous intellectual duel between transparent, shifting figures. All elements that are not directly related to chess—his brothers' wives, the grass, the shrubbery, even his brothers' beards—have disappeared. Bright colors have given way to Cubism's characteristically muted tones. Visual effects

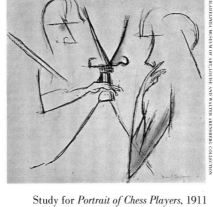

Study for *Portrait of Chess Players*, 1911

Study for *Portrait of Chess Players*, 1911

The Chess Players, 1910

Portrait of Chess Players, 1911

that had previously been unthinkable—such as chessmen seen through a player's cheek—have become an integral part of the picture. Duchamp was delighted to discover in Cubism a variety of ways to represent the essence of his favorite game; he felt that "there is a great correlation between chess and art. They say chess is a science, but it is played man against man, and that is where art comes in." The preliminary sketches shown here are but two of the many approaches he considered before he started the painting. The Puteaux Cubists were impressed by young Duchamp's work, and its display at the Salon of the Golden Section testified to their eager acceptance of him.

The Sonata, 1911

Duchamp was no more satisfied by orthodox Cubism than he had been by any earlier style of painting. In his earliest Cubist-oriented work, *The Sonata*, his direction is not yet evident: "The pale and tender tonalities of this picture," wrote critic Robert Lebel, "in which the angular contours are bathed in an evanescent atmosphere, reveal Marcel in his closest harmony with the group at Puteaux." Very different is *Yvonne and Magdeleine Torn in Tatters*. Here the Cubist concept of dissecting and fragmenting forms is used to show Duchamp's two youngest sisters, in four eerie and misshapen profiles, advancing from youth to old age.

In *Portrait*, whose bouquet of pastel shades shows the unmistakable influence of Jacques Villon's *Little Girl at the Piano (page 20)*, Duchamp uses five figures to represent a single subject—and something more. *Yvonne and Magdeleine Torn in Tatters* had depicted motion through time; now *Portrait* seemed to suggest motion through space, a concept that he would explore further in his next paintings.

Yvonne and Magdeleine Torn in Tatters, 1911

Portrait, 1911

25

Jules Etienne Marey: *Chronophotograph*, c. 1890

Sad Young Man in a Train, 1911

The first picture in which Duchamp expressly tried to represent motion was *Sad Young Man in a Train*, whose four or five successive profiles jolting across the canvas from left to right suggest the image of a passenger on a moving train. The somber colors and black borders reflect Duchamp's mood at the time; he was about to leave for Munich to escape Paris' commercialized atmosphere—but would soon be disappointed to find Munich "just another art factory."

Motion is made much more explicit in *Nude Descending a Staircase, No. 1 (right, below)*. In this first version of his most famous painting, the artist clearly shows the inspiration provided by Jules Etienne Marey's chronophotographs *(above)*, in which rapid-fire multiple exposures revealed the true dynamics of men and animals in action. In *Nude Descending a Staircase, No. 2*, he developed and refined still further the swirling lines and staccato arcs of dots that delineated the progress of his moving subject. Reaction to this painting among the Puteaux Cubists was immediate and violent, marking the end of Duchamp's formal affiliation with any group. And a year later, when it was exhibited in the New York Armory Show, American critics were equally hostile: they blasted the picture as "a collection of saddlebags," "leather, tin and broken violin," and a Chicago newspaper advised viewers to "eat three Welsh Rarebits and sniff cocaine" if they wanted to understand the painting.

Four decades later, when it had long been recognized as a masterpiece, Duchamp declared, "There's nothing to be ashamed of in it, no. . . . It is posterity, even if only a 40-year posterity, that really makes a masterpiece."

Nude Descending a Staircase, No. 1, 1911

NU DESCENDANT UN ESCALIER

Nude Descending a Staircase, No. 2, 1912

II

Through Art to Anti-Art

The modern school of painting seems to me the most audacious that has ever appeared. —GUILLAUME APOLLINAIRE

Paris in 1912 was the vortex of a thousand artistic energies that had been gathering force since 1890 or earlier. Picasso and Braque had just carried Cubism into a new phase with their invention of collage. Robert Delaunay, the French Cubist, and Frank Kupka, a transplanted Czech, were verging into Orphism, or total abstraction. In Munich, another active center of modernism, the Russian Wassily Kandinsky was simultaneously following the same course; within the next two years, Suprematism and Rayonism would break out in Russia, Vorticism in England, and, by 1917, "De Stijl" in Holland—all generated by the Cubist-Futurist ferment whose center was Paris.

The position of Duchamp at this moment was somewhat delicate. In a single painting that contained elements of both Cubism and Futurism, he had not only caught up with his own era but had gone ahead of it. Duchamp, however, lacked the temperament for competitive modernism. After the withdrawal of his *Nude Descending a Staircase* from the Indépendants exhibition he set to work on another large painting in the same manner, entitled *The King and Queen Surrounded by Swift Nudes.* The painting was preceded by a watercolor called *The King and Queen Traversed by Nudes at High Speed,* and by two pencil sketches on the same theme. Soon afterward, in July, Duchamp made his first trip outside France. He traveled alone to Munich, where he stayed for two months, working at an accelerated rate. In this brief period he completed a watercolor called *Virgin,* two masterly oils—*The Passage from the Virgin to the Bride* and *Bride*—and the first sketch for *The Bride Stripped Bare by Her Bachelors, Even,* that astonishing work to which he would devote himself for the next 10 years.

The titles of Duchamp's pictures in this climactic phase seem to suggest a movement through several stages of eroticism: nude, swift nudes, virgin, bride. Such a movement is evident in the paintings themselves. In *Nude Descending a Staircase* and *The King and Queen Surrounded by Swift Nudes (page 28),* the spectator is given an exterior view of mechanical nudity, as it were; he is a *voyeur,* looking on from the outside. With the drawing and the watercolor called *Virgin (page 84),* how-

In 1910, Duchamp painted *Paradise (above),* a realistic but rather grotesque portrayal of Adam and Eve. Two years later, having made a series of studies for a painting which critics have seen as a variation on the theme of Oedipal conflict, he turned the old canvas over and executed the new work *(left)* on its back.

The King and Queen Surrounded by Swift Nudes, 1912

ever, Duchamp provided a glimpse inside the mechanism of sex. When we come to *The Passage from the Virgin to the Bride (page 84)* and *Bride (page 85)*, we are at the heart of the mystery. The machine imagery has given way to strange, visceral forms, whose anatomical allusions are reinforced by their delicate rose, pink and oyster-white tones. Although both these paintings make use of Cubist techniques, they are not really Cubist in effect. Duchamp has entered here into his own unique realm and produced an utterly new form of painting.

Characteristically, though, Duchamp did not choose to pursue this highly original course any further. *The Passage from the Virgin to the Bride* (now in The Museum of Modern Art in New York) and *Bride* (in the Philadelphia Museum) marked the climax and virtually the close of his painting career. At the age of 25, he embarked on a new work that would finally take him out of the world of painting altogether.

Any number of explanations have been suggested for the turn taken by Duchamp's career after his return from Munich. One theory is that in *Passage* and *Bride*, Duchamp achieved such a mastery of painting technique that he sensed he was in danger of being seduced by beauty. Roberto Matta Echaurren, the Chilean painter who later became a close friend of Duchamp's, believes on the other hand that *Passage* involved him with "a whole new problem in art—to paint the moment of change, change itself," an idea so profound that to pursue it further would have required a lifetime's dedication. Since Duchamp valued his personal freedom far too highly for that, Matta says, he withdrew into a private world of mockery and ironic jokes.

The trouble with such explanations is that they ignore the very clear connection that exists between the paintings done in Munich and the gradually evolving concept of the work, first sketched out in Munich, to which Duchamp would give the provocative title, *La Mariée Mise à Nu par ses Célibataires, Même (The Bride Stripped Bare by her Bachelors, Even*—now usually referred to more simply as the *Large Glass).* This fantastically complex work will be discussed in a separate chapter. For the moment, though, it is worth noting that Duchamp originally planned it as a painting on canvas (the idea to do it on glass came later); that he referred to it in his notes as a "steam engine," which suggests a close affinity with the machinelike images of his earlier paintings; and that the whole idea of a transition from one erotic state to another, which is at the heart of *The Passage from the Virgin to the Bride,* is also the basic theme of the *Large Glass (pages 88-93).*

Whatever similarity the new project had to what had gone before, however, Duchamp certainly intended it to break new ground. "From Munich on I was finished with Cubism," he has said. "The whole trend of painting was something I didn't care to continue. . . . After Munich I tried to look for another, personal way, and of course I couldn't expect anyone to be interested in what I was doing."

Returning to Paris in September 1912, Duchamp made little effort to renew his contacts within the art world. He continued to see his brothers, of course, and even sent his controversial *Nude Descending a Staircase* to the Salon de la Section d'Or exhibition that fall. While this exhibition helped to dissolve any remaining awkwardness between the brothers Duchamp, it did not alter Marcel's decision to steer clear of groups, esthetic in-fighting, and competitive exhibitions.

Meanwhile, there remained the problem of making a living. Duchamp's paintings were not selling, and now that he was concentrating almost exclusively on the new project he had started in Munich, a project that became increasingly ambitious as time went on, there was little prospect of his earning anything from the practice of art. Duchamp's solution was to take a job in 1913 as a library clerk in the Bibliothèque Sainte-Geneviève. The salary, though minute, was sufficient to cover his modest needs. The work was relatively undemanding, and it left him plenty of free time to devote to the new project—the development of which consisted at this point mainly of intellectual and verbal ideas that he jotted down, in a kind of personal, poetic shorthand, on scraps of paper that he preserved in a green cardboard box.

Duchamp's closest companions during this period were the mercurial Picabia and the equally flamboyant Guillaume Apollinaire, who had already set his mark upon the epoch. The illegitimate son of a tempestuous, Polish-born mother and an Italian father (whom he often liked to identify vaguely as a high Vatican official, at *least* a Cardinal), Apollinaire was a volatile, exuberant, brilliantly gifted poet who had come to Paris about 1900 and soon established himself as the principal spokesman for the new movement, or, as he called it, the "new spirit" in the arts. Like Baudelaire, who also wrote art criticism, Apollinaire was a poet deeply interested in painting. He knew all the important artists, served as a link between the various groups and factions, coined a great many of the names by which the new movements became known (including the terms Orphism, Simultaneism, and Surrealism) and not only participated in but created many of the legends of that legendary time. His energy was boundless, his high spirits indestructible. The year before, he had been falsely accused of the sensational theft of the Mona Lisa from the Louvre; he spent six terrible days in Paris' Santé prison before his innocence could be established, and his friends feared that the scandal would wreck his career. Apollinaire, however, resumed his tidal outpouring of reviews, pamphlets, and poetry, and within a year had regained his position as the most influential critic in Paris. When he and Duchamp first met, in 1912, Apollinaire was getting ready to publish his *Aesthetic Meditations: The Cubist Painters*, a work that played a major role in the triumph of the new painting.

Apollinaire could scarcely have found a more stimulating pair than Picabia and Duchamp, who occupied themselves in keeping open what Duchamp once called a "corridor of humor" through the dense thickets of art theory. Picabia's humor was farcical and savage; Duchamp's was quietly diabolical. Their conversations, which gave free rein to every imaginative flight and fancy, were studded with the constant clash of wit and paradox. In her memoirs of the period, Picabia's wife, Gabrielle Buffet-Picabia, wrote that the two "emulated one another in their extraordinary adherence to paradoxical, destructive principles, in their blasphemies and inhumanities which were directed not only against the old myths of art, but against all the foundations of life in general. . . . Better than by any rational method, they thus pursued the disintegration of the concept of art, substituting a personal dynamism . . . for the codified values of formal Beauty." As Mme. Buffet-Picabia shrewdly observed, these "forays of demoralization," in which Apollinaire often took part, foreshadowed a state of mind that would later assume a more public form in the phenomenon of Dada.

If Duchamp's "corridor of humor" led straight to Dada, it also extended back to an earlier generation of French iconoclasts. The break with the spirit of gravity in French literature was clearly evident in the fantastic novels and plays of Alfred Jarry, who had electrified Paris in 1896 with his wildly satirical farce-drama *Ubu Roi*, and who then proceeded to assume in his own life the pompously ceremonial speech and mannerisms of his protagonist, the political monster, Père Ubu. Jarry also founded and promulgated the new science of 'Pataphysics, which he defined as the science of the laws that govern exceptions. The so-called "laws" of science were not really laws at all, he maintained, but merely exceptions that occurred more frequently than others; 'Pataphysicians accordingly rejected all scientific explanations of any kind, argued that everything could just as well be its opposite, and formulated axioms such as Jarry's famous "DEFINITION: God is the shortest distance between zero and infinity . . . in either direction."

Even before Jarry, the composer Erik Satie had been injecting the humor of absurdity into music. Satie's "humoristic" compositions, with their whimsical titles ("Cold Pieces," "Three Pieces in the Form of a Pear") and their ironic instructions to the performer—one phrase was to be sung "like a nightingale with a toothache"—were in one sense pure distillations of his shy, quirky personality, which also expressed itself in odd little prose fragments. "Why attack God?" Satie wrote. "He is as unhappy as we are. Since his son's death he has no appetite for anything, and barely nibbles at his food." But in another sense all Satie's work can be seen as a veiled attack on the overblown rhetorical bombast of German music, especially Wagner's, from which the French composers were trying to free themselves.

Duchamp and Picabia were well aware of this current of humor that pushed toward the absurd. Satie had started to compose again about 1910, after a long lapse, and was later to be held in great esteem by the group of young avant-garde composers in Paris who were known as *Les Six*. Jarry had died in 1907 of poverty and alcoholism, but his blundering, grotesque creation Père Ubu lived on, exercising a strange fascination over writers as dissimilar as André Breton and André Gide. The spirit of Jarry, moreover, showed up unmistakably in the writings of Raymond Roussel, whom Duchamp greatly admired. Roussel was another eccentric genius, a recluse with an independent income that enabled him to wander about Europe at will, playing chess and writing extraordinary novels in which the most improbable events were recounted in a deadpan style that made great use of puns and the totally illogical association of like-sounding words. A performance of Roussel's play *Impressions d'Afrique*, in Paris in 1911, seems to have made a

© 1961 NEW DIRECTIONS

Alfred Jarry's sketch of his bizarre hero Ubu Roi *(above)* was made for a published version of the play of the same name. Duchamp, who was fascinated by Jarry's writings, designed a leather binding for a 1935 edition of the play *(below)*, cleverly incorporating the title itself.

PHILADELPHIA MUSEUM OF ART, THE LOUISE AND WALTER ARENSBERG COLLECTION

strong impression on Duchamp. The play lasted only one night and was incomprehensible to most of the few people who were present. But Duchamp has said that it "showed me the way," and directly influenced the conception of *The Bride Stripped Bare by Her Bachelors, Even*.

Ever since Munich, this work had been evolving on two different planes—one visual and one purely verbal. Its verbal, "literary" aspect took the form of written notations for ideas whose visual realization Duchamp would then sketch out on the plaster wall of his Paris studio. If the real basis of the work was verbal, though, it should be emphasized that Duchamp's verbal ideas followed a logic all their own. Duchamp had no more respect than Roussel for the 18th Century rationalism that had set the standards of French prose and engendered the famous French clarity of expression. What he did admire was the strange power he had found in the work of such poets as Mallarmé and Rimbaud, a power that enabled words to break free of accustomed meanings and operate in a new, nonrational context. "Words get their real meaning in poetry," he said once. Moreover, Duchamp had always delighted in puns and alliterative word play. His discovery of Roussel encouraged him to go much further along these lines.

Verbal logic, however, was by no means the sole target of Duchamp's irony. At a time when many of the Cubists were obsessed with trying to apply the most recent discoveries of science and mathematics in their work, Duchamp undertook, like Jarry, to question the ultimate validity of science in general. Why should the "laws" of science be revered, any more than the "laws" of language or art? The word law was against his principles. Scientific laws, he argued, were merely convenient ways of explaining phenomena that man's limited intelligence had failed to grasp—a situation attested to by the fact that "every 50 years or so a new law is discovered that invalidates the old one."

In this spirit, Duchamp began to invent a new "playful physics" of his own, based on such concepts as "oscillating density," "emancipated metal" and the "adage of spontaneity," all of which he applied in his work on the *Large Glass*. He also decided that this work would be four-dimensional. The scientific idea of a fourth dimension, which the Paris artists liked to discuss at great length, underwent in Duchamp's mind the customary ironic twist. Duchamp decided that the ideal fourth-dimensional situation was the physical act of love, "which is why love has been so much respected." *The Bride Stripped Bare by Her Bachelors, Even* would thus be the graphic expression, on the highest level of pseudo-science, of the fourth-dimensional phenomenon of sex.

In his book *The Cubist Painters*, published in 1913, Apollinaire made a curious observation about his friend Duchamp. "Perhaps," he wrote, "it will be the task of an artist as detached from esthetic preoccupations, and as intent on the energetic as Marcel Duchamp, to reconcile art and the people." Duchamp always considered this statement ridiculous, and it was soon to be proved premature, at least, by events on the other side of the Atlantic. In February 1913, the Armory Show opened in New York, giving Americans their first horrified look at Cubism and other aspects of the "new spirit" in European art. From the outset,

The Rude Descending a Staircase
(Rush Hour at the Subway)

Newspaper cartoonists had a field day with
the Armory Show. One *(above)* saw
Duchamp's *Nude* as inspired by the subway
rush hour. Another insisted that the old
ladies who made patchwork quilts originated
Cubism. The soundest comment came from
an editorial writer who warned, "You can't
spoof what you don't understand."

THE ORIGINAL CUBIST

the outraged guardians of public taste singled out Duchamp's *Nude
Descending a Staircase* as the prime example of Cubist madness.

Today it is somewhat difficult to understand why the painting should
have been considered so shocking. Duchamp himself was inclined to
think that the title caused most of the trouble. In traditional art,
nudes stood or reclined; they had never before come down a flight of
stairs. Whatever the reason, people stood in line to see the picture
that had been caricatured by newspaper cartoonists and damned by
the critics, one of whom called it "an explosion in a shingle factory."

If the people in general were not ready to be reconciled, there were
still a few enterprising collectors and dealers who recognized the new
spirit as a force to be reckoned with, and who bought up most of the
European paintings in the show (the American works did not fare as
well, and American painting was never the same afterward). A San
Francisco dealer named F. C. Torrey paid $324 for *Nude Descending a
Staircase*. Duchamp had sent three other paintings over for the show—
Portrait of Chess Players, *Sad Young Man on a Train*, and *The King and
Queen Surrounded by Swift Nudes*—and all three of them were sold,
too, bringing the artist an unexpected windfall of about $970 in all.
Picabia, who had gone to New York for the opening, returned with
fabulous accounts of the triumph. Duchamp listened to Picabia's sto-
ries with great interest, but he showed not the slightest inclination to
exploit the new market.

By the spring of 1913, Duchamp's course was taking him farther and
farther away from the preoccupations and problems of his fellow artists. Retinal art, art for the eye alone, interested him less than ever. He
was determined to break out of the retinal trap, and in order to do that
he felt he had to remove from his own work all traces of what used to be
called in French *la patte*—the artist's personal style, his touch, his
"paw." One way to do this, he decided, would be to execute the new
work on glass rather than on canvas.

The idea came to him one day when he happened to be using a sheet
of glass for a palette; looking through at the colors from the underside,
he was struck with the thought that a painting on glass could be sealed
hermetically, which would prevent or at least delay the gradual oxidation that causes pigments to fade and change color. Even better, the use
of an unfamiliar medium like glass should help him to get away from
"painterly" traditions. But how could he get rid of *la patte?* The problem was to find a new method of drawing, and Duchamp's solution was
brilliantly simple: he borrowed from engineering the technique of mechanical drawing, in which "you are directed by the impersonality of
the ruler." Obvious as it sounds now, the idea was a major breakthrough. "It's very difficult to escape from the prison of tradition,"
Duchamp said once. "Education is so strong, it holds you like a chain.
I didn't get completely free even then, but I tried—I unlearned to
draw. I had to forget *with my hand*."

In addition to the schematic drawing on the wall of his studio, Duchamp carried out several studies for the *Large Glass* during 1913 and
1914. The first, entitled *Chocolate Grinder*, was a small painting on

canvas of an actual chocolate grinder that he had often seen in the window of a chocolate shop in Rouen; Duchamp depicted it just as it was, with three interlocking drums on a platform supported by elegant little Louis XV legs. This would later become a central organ of the Bachelor Machine in the *Glass*. It was followed by a second version in which the radial lines of the grinding drums, instead of being painted, were made by gluing and sewing white thread to the canvas *(page 85)*. Soon afterward, Duchamp started experimenting with various methods of painting on glass. His first efforts involved the use of paraffin and fluoridic acid as an engraving medium, but the fumes from the acid were so strong that he gave it up. Then he tried outlining his design in fine lead wire. This worked perfectly: it kept the colors in place, and it could be stretched out to make a line as straight and impersonal as any drawn by a ruler. The method required infinite pains, but Duchamp was satisfied. He finished a small study on glass for the *Glider*, or *Sleigh*, section of the Bachelor Machine, using the lead wire technique *(page 91)*, and started work on the *Malic Molds (page 87)* that were to be the images of the Bachelors.

At the same time, his sense of humor found vent in a number of decidedly unusual and somewhat subversive activities. Why, Duchamp asked himself, should one accept as immutably valid the standard unit of measurement, the meter, which was based on a platinum-iridium bar stored in a vault in a Paris suburb? He decided to make his own units of measurement, based on the laws of chance.

Paying precise attention to each detail in the approved scientific manner, he cut three pieces of thread exactly one meter in length, dropped each one from a height of one meter upon a long, narrow stretched canvas painted Prussian blue, and bonded them to the canvas with varnish in the shape they had assumed. The three canvases were cut from their stretchers and glued down to glass plates. When Duchamp decided to incorporate these "new forms to the unit of length" in his *Large Glass*, he had three wooden rulers cut from draftsman's straight edges so as to conform exactly to the curves of the dropped threads, and used them as templates. He eventually enshrined the mounted threads and rulers in a box of the type that was used to hold croquet mallets. These were the *Three Standard Stoppages*. They would figure prominently in the *Large Glass* and in several other works, the first of which was a painting, dated 1914, called *Network of Stoppages (pages 86-87)*, in which he superimposed the lines of the *Three Standard Stoppages* on an earlier painting called *Young Man and Girl in Spring*.

The whole idea of chance, which would assume such importance in 20th Century art, interested Duchamp primarily as an alternative to the "laws" of science. Unlike many later artists, though, who saw in chance a way to get beyond their own personal taste, Duchamp always thought of it as an expression of each individual's subconscious personality. "Your chance is not the same as mine," he once explained, "just as your throw of the dice will rarely be the same as mine."

Even more subversive, from the point of view of subsequent art history, were the three objects that appeared in Duchamp's studio dur-

Always delighted with the frivolous and unpredictable nature of chance, Duchamp, one day in 1913, amused himself and two sisters by using it to compose a piece of music. Writing notes on bits of paper, Duchamp, Yvonne and Magdeleine jumbled them in a bag and then drew them out at random, writing the notes on music paper as they appeared. Duchamp happily called this exercise in chance *Musical Erratum*.

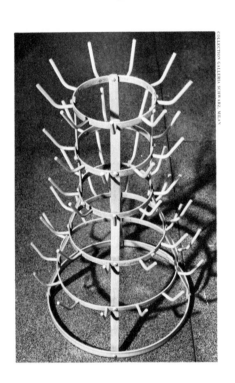

Bottle Rack was one of Duchamp's first readymades. Purchased in a Paris department store in 1914, it represented for Duchamp the possibilities of "solving an artistic problem without the usual means or processes." Like most of his readymades, the original *Bottle Rack* was inscribed, but it has been lost and Duchamp does not remember what he wrote. The version above is one of eight duplicates made in 1964 for an Italian art dealer and is signed by Duchamp.

ing this period. The first of these was the front wheel of a bicycle, which Duchamp mounted upside down, by its fork, on a kitchen stool, so that a touch of the hand would set it spinning. Duchamp has said that there was no particular idea in his mind when he did this, and that he just acquired the wheel as a pleasant gadget. Soon afterward, in January 1914, he bought in an art supply store a cheap chromolithograph of a particularly insipid winter landscape, added one red and one green blob of color to the background (the color of the bottles placed in druggists' windows), and called the result *Pharmacy*. Some Duchamp disciples have interpreted the title as a sarcastic reference to his sister Suzanne's marriage to a pharmacist, but Duchamp had another explanation: *Pharmacy*, he said, was simply "a distortion of the visual idea to execute an intellectual idea," something wrenched out of one context and placed arbitrarily in a new and unfamiliar one.

The process of distortion showed even more clearly in the third object, which appeared later in 1914. This was a galvanized iron rack for drying wine bottles, an inexpensive household item that Duchamp bought in a store and to which he signed his name. The mere act of signing it served to wrench this object out of the "useful" context and placed it, derisively, in the context of a "work of art." Duchamp seemed to be implying that anything made by man or by man's machines was art, and that the artist was merely someone who signed things.

The *Bottle Rack* of 1914 was thus in a sense a quietly diabolical attack on the whole tradition of Western art, and its reverberations have carried right down to the present day. All these objects, which in the following year received the generic name "readymade," were defined once and for all in 1934 by the Surrealist leader André Breton, who called them "manufactured objects promoted to the dignity of objects of art through the choice of the artist."

While Duchamp quietly undermined several centuries of Western art with his readymades, Europe accelerated its own plunge toward destruction. The final breakup of the old order was now at hand; one by one, the artists went off to experience in the front lines the destruction that they had prefigured in their art.

Apollinaire volunteered for duty, although as an Italian citizen he was not liable for service. He was rejected at first, but later managed to get a lieutenant's commission and served in the French Army with distinction. Picabia, who loved fast cars, became the chauffeur to a general. Picasso, the Spaniard, saw his friend Braque off to the front; they would never again work closely together. Léger donned the poilu's uniform, as did Jacques Villon and Raymond Duchamp-Villon. The superheated martial atmosphere of Paris soon became increasingly difficult for their brother Marcel, who, having served for one year in 1906, was now judged unfit for military duty because of a weak heart. Duchamp rarely ever speaks of those days in 1914 when his youthful good looks and civilian clothes drew their daily quota of insults from ultra-patriotic citizens. From such experiences he conceived a bitterness against his countrymen that would last for many years, although he never showed it. When the American painter Walter Pach, who had played a key role in collecting the European art for the Armory Show, arrived in Paris early in 1915 and suggested that Duchamp come to the United States, no further urging was needed. Duchamp booked third-class passage aboard the *Rochambeau*, which sailed for New York in June.

He was rather surprised to find himself famous upon arrival. America had not forgotten the shock of *Nude Descending a Staircase*, and in New York Duchamp's reputation as a Frenchman was equaled, according to his fellow countryman Henri-Pierre Roché, "only by Napoleon and Sarah Bernhardt." His lionization began the moment his ship docked, when he was met at the pier by a delegation of reporters whose clamorous questions he answered, through an interpreter, with what one newsman described as "smiling composure."

New York at this time was the center of an extremely active avant-garde group that included the American painters Walter Pach, Charles Demuth, Marsden Hartley and Joseph Stella; the Walter C. Arensbergs, wealthy collectors of the most advanced art; Katherine S. Dreier, a strong-willed heiress who had also started collecting modern art after her conversion to it at the Armory Show; and a growing number of Europeans cast up by the War—Albert Gleizes, Jean Crotti, Marius de Zayas, Edgard Varèse, and later on Picabia, who had arranged to have himself sent on a military mission to buy molasses in Cuba (a mission that he forgot all about when he reached New York). At the center of this lively circle was Alfred Stieglitz, the great pioneer photographer, whose gallery at 291 Fifth Avenue had become a center for the development and display of the most advanced tendencies in the arts a good five years before the Armory Show gave them wider currency. Stieglitz's magazine, *291*, published in 1915, carried reproductions of Cubist and other advanced works, and Stieglitz himself constantly encouraged his artist friends to break decisively with the old representational traditions in art—traditions that had been permanently undermined by the invention of photography.

Duchamp and Picabia became the brightest stars of this glittering circle. They both loved the free and easy atmosphere of New York, the absence of esthetic traditions, the openhanded friendliness shown on all sides. Formerly somewhat shy and retiring, Duchamp now plunged enthusiastically into the continual round of parties and gatherings, many of which took place at Stieglitz's or at the Arensberg apartment at 33 West 67th Street where, as Gabrielle Buffet-Picabia put it, "at any hour of the day or night one was sure of finding sandwiches, first-class chess players, and an atmosphere entirely free from conventional and social prejudices." Chronicles of the period all stress Duchamp's extraordinary charm and his physical attractiveness. Scores of young women appear to have fallen frantically in love with him, bewitched by the finely chiseled features of this handsome, reddish-blond Norman who looked almost more American than French, and beguiled by his irrepressible gaiety and irreverent wit. Roché, a well-connected young Frenchman who met Duchamp in New York early in 1916, has written that Duchamp "could have had his choice of heiresses, but he preferred to play chess and live on the proceeds of the exclusive

French lessons he gave for two dollars an hour. He was an enigma, contrary to all tradition, and he won everybody's heart."

The French lessons took the place of the librarian's job in Paris. His pupils were often well-to-do admirers like the Stettheimer sisters, Florine and Ettie, and Duchamp often said that he learned more English from his pupils than they learned French. The modest profits gave him enough to live on, for living was cheap and Duchamp did not have to pay rent—Walter Arensberg had provided him with a studio at 33 West 67th Street, in exchange for which Duchamp promised to give him the *Large Glass* when it was finished. He had started to work on the *Glass* soon after his arrival, buying two large sheets of heavy plate glass and installing them on sawhorses in his studio, where each day he continued the slow, infinitely painstaking process of re-creating the ideas and images that had all been sketched out on the wall of his Paris studio. He spent a year on the upper panel, which depicted the Bride, before turning his attention to the Bachelor apparatus that would form the work's lower half. He worked for two hours a day, seldom more. "There was the fact of my laziness," he said once. "I've never been able to work more than two hours a day. And then, you see, it interested me but not enough to be *eager* to finish it. I was just doing it, that was my life, but I also wanted to see America."

From time to time a new readymade appeared in his studio. The first American readymade was a snow shovel that he bought in a hardware store on Columbus Avenue, signed, and suspended from the ceiling. He called it *In Advance of the Broken Arm (page 39)*. This was followed by *Comb*, a metal comb of the type used in grooming animals, along the back of which Duchamp had inscribed, in French, "Three or four drops of height have nothing to do with savagery." "The thing was to write something that had nothing to do with dogs or combs," Duchamp explained, "something as nonsensical as possible." *With Hidden Noise* consisted of a ball of twine compressed between two metal plates bearing a cryptographic inscription; at his own suggestion, Walter Arensberg placed a small object known only to himself inside the ball of twine, so that when the contraption was shaken it made a sound. Other readymades, dating from 1917, include *Apolinère Enameled*, an advertisement for Sapolin enamel paint which Duchamp altered slightly to honor his friend Apollinaire; *Traveler's Folding Item*, the dust cover for an Underwood typewriter; *Hat Rack*, a wooden hat rack; and *Trap*, or *Trébuchet*, a coat rack screwed to the floor of his studio so he or his guests might occasionally trip over it.

All these bizarre items, in their offhand way, reflected the notion of taking a common object out of its customary setting and placing it, verbally or visually or both, in a new and unfamiliar one. The readymade itself could simply be selected (like *Hat Rack* and *Traveler's Folding Item*), or it could be "assisted" by the artist (*With Hidden Noise, Apolinère Enameled*). Each one of them really carried a "hidden noise" in the form of a wicked little Bronx cheer directed at the seriousness of high art. Duchamp was very careful, however, not to let them turn into an artistic activity. He made a note to himself to limit the

In addition to the readymades which Duchamp elevated to art by signing, he made others by slightly altering the original. Above is an advertisement for Sapolin Enamel which he changed to make a pun on the name of the poet Apollinaire. He also signed and dated it, adding the inscription "Any Act Red by her Ten or Epergne, New York, U.S.A.," which has been interpreted as a reference to the Bride in the *Large Glass*. As usual, Duchamp refused to clarify.

number of readymades yearly, and he never sold them; they remained in his studio or were given away to friends. When three readymades were included in an exhibition at the Bourgeois Gallery in New York in 1916, Duchamp insisted that they be hung unceremoniously from a coat rack at the gallery door, where, to his unfeigned delight, nobody even noticed them.

The sardonic attitude that produced the readymades was also becoming more and more evident in the work of other artists of this period. Picabia, who had managed to get himself discharged from the Army on medical grounds, had started painting pictures of mechanical devices that bore blatantly derisive titles. *Portrait of an American Girl in a State of Nudity*, for example, depicted a large spark plug with an inscription underneath reading "FOR EVER." Another young painter, with whom Duchamp had been on close terms since 1915, the diminutive and eccentric Man Ray (born in Philadelphia in 1890) had begun under Duchamp's influence to turn out anti-art objects whose sly wit was uniquely his own. Ray's 1919 *Lampshade* was a white spiral made from an unrolled lampshade. *Cadeau*, the most famous of Man Ray's objects, was a flatiron with a row of sharp tacks glued to the underside.

The spirit behind all these "machine style" paintings and objects was very close to the spirit that animated the group of young European War refugees who had come together by chance in Zurich, and who were at that very moment launching the Dada movement. Dada from its inception took the form of highly aggressive public action—something that could not be said of the readymades. However, Duchamp's New York activities were showing an increasingly aggressive tendency; before taking temporary leave of Duchamp to trace the frenetic rise and fall of Dada, it is worth recalling a well-known provocative gesture by Duchamp that was clearly Dadaistic in character.

The Society of Independent Artists, which Duchamp had helped to found in New York, put on an exhibition in 1917 that was open to any artist who paid the six-dollar fee. There was no jury, and, theoretically, at least, no restrictions on what could be shown. Duchamp, who had helped with the hanging, decided to test the reality of this artistic freedom. He bought from a plumbing supply firm a porcelain urinal, which he christened *Fountain* and sent in with the requisite fee, under the name of "R. Mutt." The hanging committee indignantly refused to exhibit this item as sculpture. Duchamp argued the case later in *The Blind Man*, an ephemeral little magazine financed by Arensberg and Roché and edited by Duchamp, and in doing so he provided his own succinct definition of the readymade work of art. "Whether Mr. Mutt with his own hands made the fountain or not has no importance," Duchamp wrote. "He CHOSE it. He took an ordinary article of life, placed it so that its useful significance disappeared under a new title and point of view—[he] created a new thought for that object."

As for the committee's objections on moral grounds, Duchamp dismissed those as being absurd. "It is a fixture that you see every day in plumbers' show windows," he noted. Besides which, "The only works of art America has given [us] are her plumbing and her bridges."

Two of Duchamp's most famous readymades were a snow shovel and a plumbing fixture. The shovel was called *In Advance of the Broken Arm* and signed by the artist. *Fountain*, on the other hand, was signed with the pseudonym "R. Mutt" and stoutly defended by Duchamp on behalf of "Mr. Mutt" when the Society of Independent Artists refused to exhibit it.

The Pine Tree Flag of the American Revolution, seen superimposed on a photograph of New York's 69th Regiment Armory, symbolized "The New Spirit" that the Armory Show engendered in American art.

The Show That Shook America

That's not art!" roared Theodore Roosevelt. "Insanity," cried the critics. What stirred their wrath was the 1913 International Exhibition of Modern Art—the epic New York Armory Show that gave America its first comprehensive look at the explosive new art of Europe. A public that had been brought up on a diet of strict representational art was abruptly confronted with a host of "stranger things than you ever dreamed were on land or sea," as photographer Alfred Stieglitz wrote in a newspaper article before the show. A moving power in the exhibit, Stieglitz was the first to exhibit works by Rodin, Matisse, Picasso and other revolutionaries in his own gallery at 291 Fifth Avenue. He was convinced that photography would inevitably replace realistic painting as an art form of its own, and he felt that American art desperately needed a transfusion of fresh ideas and techniques if it was ever to achieve greatness.

And a transfusion it did indeed receive. Although the New York Realists were in the majority, the Europeans stole the show. Only one third of the 1,300-odd works exhibited were theirs. These caused all the commotion, comprised 80 per cent of the sales and received virtually all the publicity. After the exhibition closed, the *Tribune* critic Royal Cortissoz wrote: "It was a good show, but don't do it again." His jest was unnecessary. There could not be another show like this one—the bombshell had exploded, and American art would never again be the same.

INTERNATIONAL EXHIBITION
MODERN ART

INTERNATIONAL EXHIBITION
OF MODERN ART
ASSOCIATION OF AMERICAN
PAINTERS AND SCULPTORS
69th INF'T'Y REGT ARMORY, NEW YORK CITY
FEBRUARY 15th TO MARCH 15th 1913
AMERICAN & FOREIGN ART.

AMONG THE GUESTS WILL BE — INGRES, DELACROIX, DEGAS,
CÉZANNE, REDON, RENOIR, MONET, SEURAT, VAN GOGH,
HODLER, SLEVOGT, JOHN, PRYDE, SICKERT, MAILLOL,
BRANCUSI, LEHMBRUCK, BERNARD, MATISSE, MANET, SIGNAC,
LAUTREC, CONDER, DENIS, RUSSELL, DUFY, BRAQUE, HERBIN,
GLEIZES, SOUZA-CARDOZO, ZAK, DU CHAMP-VILLON,
GAUGUIN, ARCHIPENKO, BOURDELLE, C. DE SEGONZAC.
LEXINGTON AVE.–25th ST.

Magazine Section
Part Six

The New

SUNDAY.

"CUBISTS AND FUTURISTS

E MAKING INSANITY PAY"

The Armory Show was, in many respects, more like a three-ring circus than an art exhibition. Its sponsoring body, the Association of American Painters and Sculptors, was well aware of the furor that would be created: upwards of 120,000 catalogues, pamphlets and post cards were printed, and the newspapers were deluged with press releases. The effort paid off handsomely: satirical cartoons, provocative headlines and scathing reviews brought out larger crowds than had ever attended any art event. "Have these 'progressives' really outstripped . . . us, glimpsed the future, and used a form of artistic expression that is simply esoteric to the great laggard public?" asked critic Kenyon Cox in a *New York Times* article accompanying the banner headline shown above. "Is their work a conspicuous milestone in the progress of art? Or is it junk?" The rest of the article was devoted to the thesis that it was junk.

Many of the works in the show were subsequently viewed by nearly 13,000 visitors in Boston and 200,000 in Chicago. They were largely attracted by headlines like the following from the *Chicago Record-Herald:* "May Bar Youngsters From Cubists' Show; Instructor Declares Exhibit Is Nasty, Lewd, Immoral and Indecent." The Illinois Senatorial Vice Commission even included the exhibit in its annual vice probe. The commission's investigator quickly concluded that it was immoral: not only had he seen young girls sneaking glances at Cubist nudes, but he discovered, to his horror, that one of Matisse's nudes only had four toes.

Interior of the 1913 Armory Show

43

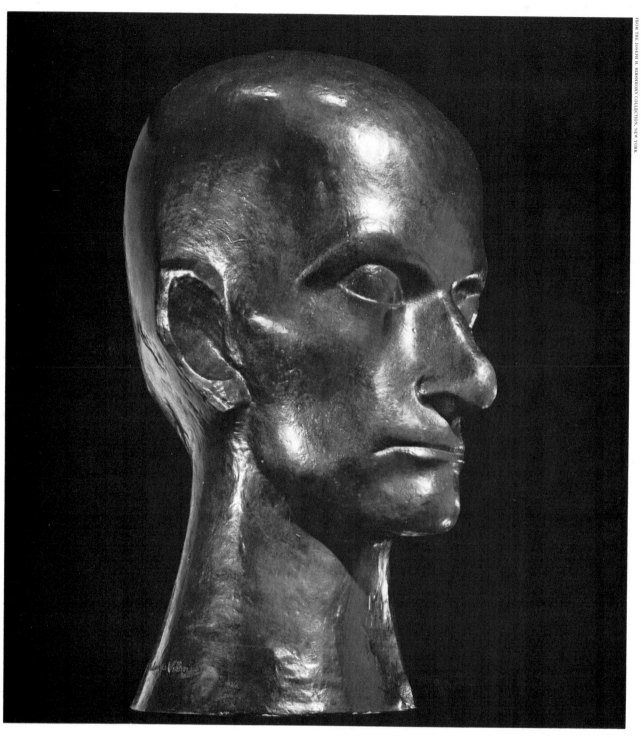

Raymond Duchamp-Villon: *Baudelaire*, 1911

The foreign sculpture shown at the Armory proved no less startling to American eyes than the paintings. The greatest hilarity was produced by Brancusi's *Mlle. Pogany* (shown at right in a later, slightly more abstract version). It was dubbed "The Duck Egg Muse," and a droll ostrich farmer sent a telegram requesting that it be reserved as "a nest egg for our hatchery."

If Brancusi's work looked too outlandish to suit the public, Raymond Duchamp-Villon's bust of Baudelaire *(above)* may have appeared too conventional: it scarcely attracted any attention at all. In fact, it was anything but conventional—this was the piece in which the sculptor first attempted to define his subject in the simple but powerful planes of Cubism. To enhance its bold lines, he even took the liberty of divesting Baudelaire of hair. Although Duchamp-Villon considered this among his most satisfying and important works, it was not sold until after he had died from World War I injuries.

Constantin Brancusi: *Mlle. Pogany,* 19

Besides reflecting on the state of American art, the 1913 Show exposed American criticism as being narrow-minded and archaic. Cézanne, Gauguin and Matisse had been revered as masters in Europe for years, but this did not faze hostile American critics. Kenyon Cox, as memorable for his conservative reviews as for his sweetly sentimental murals, attacked Gauguin as "a decorator tainted with insanity . . . always unnecessarily false and often unpleasantly morbid." Gauguin fared little better at the hands of the cataloguers: the price of $40,500 placed on the painting below seemed so unlikely to them that they concluded it was

an error and blithely reduced it to $4,050. Cézanne was called "an idiot . . . absolutely without talent . . . cut off from tradition . . . hopeless." Nonetheless, *The Poorhouse on the Hill (right, below)* was bought by The Metropolitan Museum of Art, the first Cézanne to enter any American museum.

Matisse's *Blue Nude (right)* triggered a torrent of maledictions. Critics proclaimed that Matisse's work was "leering effrontery," and that "among all these painters there is none whose work appears as perfectly childish, crude and amateurish." *Blue Nude* so incensed a mob of Chicago students that they hanged Matisse in effigy.

Paul Gauguin: *Still Life with Head-Shaped Vase and Japanese Woodcut*, 1889

Henri Matisse: *Blue Nude,* 1907

Paul Cézanne: *The Poorhouse on the Hill,* 1877

The Cubist sections of the Armory Show invariably drew the most vociferous crowds. All the Cubists came under collective attack from no less a personage than ex-President Theodore Roosevelt: "There is no reason," he wrote, "why people should not call themselves Cubists, or Octagonists, Parallelopipedonists, or Knights of the Isosceles Triangle, or Brothers of the Cosine, if they so desire; as expressing anything serious and permanent, one term is as fatuous as another."

Critical attack centered on Duchamp's *Nude Descending a Staircase (page 27)*, which had become so firmly entrenched in the public mind as the symbol of Cubist madness that other important Cubists, such as Albert Gleizes and Robert Delaunay, were all but

Albert Gleizes: *Man on a Balcony*, 1912

Francis Picabia: *Dances at the Spring*, 1912

ignored. Even Picasso and Braque, without whom there
would have been no Cubism, received surprisingly
little notice. But one Cubist who got all the attention
he could handle was Duchamp's friend Francis Picabia,
the only Cubist actually at the Armory Show. Some
uninformed reporters took his presence to mean that
the wild young Picabia was the official spokesman for
Cubism—an impression that he gleefully failed to
correct. He granted interviews and even wrote an article
for the *New York World* in which he tried to clarify
Cubism. It was filled with brain-wrenching phrases like
"the objectivity of a subjectivity," and the baffled editors
offered a prize to anyone who could "translate"
the article. The prize: a Cubist drawing.

Pablo Picasso: *Woman with Mustard Pot*, 1910

Robert Delaunay: *City of Paris*, 1910-1912

The most revolutionary painter at the Armory —though not even the most advanced supporters of the Europeans realized it at the time—was the Russian Wassily Kandinsky, represented by his *Improvisation No. 27* (purchased by the visionary Alfred Stieglitz for $550). All the other paintings, even the most wildly fractured Cubist works, were based on some sort of model. But Kandinsky's *Improvisation* was not intended to represent anything specific. It was an abstraction derived entirely from images that Kandinsky said originated in his unconscious mind—a technique that would assume major importance in the "psychic automatism" of Surrealism in the 1920s. This nonrepresentational technique was further underscored by his choice of titles: various series of Kandinsky's paintings between 1910 and 1914 were called *Improvisations*, *Compositions* and *Abstractions*.

It has been said that above all else, Kandinsky was a Russian. His enthusiasm for Russian folk art and icons is reflected in the radiant colors of his paintings. Among the sources of his inspiration for his abstractions was the breathtaking sight of the sunset over Moscow.

Wassily Kandinsky: *Improvisation No. 27*, 1912

51

wo days before the Armory Show opened, the artist and teacher Robert Henri, leader of the New York Realists, who in their own way were revolutionizing American art, walked slowly through the French section. He was visibly shaken by what he saw. He chanced to meet his close friend and former student Walter Pach, one of the show's organizers. "I hope that for every French picture that is sold," Henri said, "you sell an American one." But he already knew too well what Pach's reply would be: "That's not the proportion of merit."

Although Henri and his disciples often chose academic subjects—nudes, portraits, landscapes—they rejected the academicians' idealized view of the world; the candor and realism with which they depicted their subjects, such as the sporting events that George Bellows immortalized, were to earn for them the title "The Ashcan School." And now this new American realism had come face to face with the modern European movement.

The only one to emerge unscathed was Maurice Prendergast, an American Post-Impressionist. But Henri and Bellows, who continued to paint in the same old styles, were soon ousted from their positions in the vanguard of American art by more adventurous modernists like John Marin and Marsden Hartley. Within a few years the Realists disbanded forever; realism as a creative force in American art had become obsolete.

Robert Henri: *The Spanish Gypsy*, 1912

Maurice Prendergast: *Landscape with Figures*, 1913

George Bellows: *Polo Crowd*, 1910

54

III

The Nightmare
Cry of Dada

It is a rare gift of God to be present at the birth of a religion, or of any idea which later conquers the world. —RICHARD HUELSENBECK

By the spring of 1916—the spring of Verdun—the slaughter in the West had exceeded anything previously known in the history of war. Not even poison gas could surpass the lunatic horror of trench warfare, in which tens of thousands died to gain a few yards of scorched ground and the survivors then waited numbly for the counterattack that would drive them back. In the front lines, the words victory and defeat had lost their meaning. It is no coincidence that the Dada movement was born in that nightmare year, 1916. Viewed against the logic of the trenches, the organized insanity of Dada could be considered inevitable.

The origins of the movement extend back beyond 1914, of course, although just how far back depends somewhat upon the historian's viewpoint. Those who emphasize Dada's political character tend to point out its affinities with the anarchist disorders that swept Europe during the 1880s. Others have sought its roots in the French literary tradition of esthetic revolt, a tradition that began with Romantic poets like Chateaubriand and de Musset, was continued by Baudelaire, reached its apotheosis in the person of Arthur Rimbaud (who abandoned poetry altogether at the age of 21 and became a gun-runner in the African interior), and then took a startling new turn in the macabre and absurd humor of Alfred Jarry. Both interpretations are justified but insufficient. Dada also borrowed elements from Futurism and nearly every other vanguard art movement of the time, while cultivating with respect to all art values a total indifference which, as Tristan Tzara once noted, was not modern at all. At the very beginning, though, the Dadaist revolt was clearly and specifically a revolt against the War. Horrified and disgusted by the carnage, this polyglot band of youthful idealists fled their own warring countries and came together in the neutral town of Zurich, Switzerland, where the roar of the cannon could no longer drown out their individualistic protests.

Hugo Ball, a German conscientious objector, arrived in Zurich early in 1915. A tall, gangling, intense youth who had some experience as a stage manager, Ball conceived the idea of starting a cabaret at which he and other young artists and intellectuals could perform, show their

One of the earliest Dada works, Jean Arp's wood relief, composed of bright, free-flowing shapes, represents a tree, the moon and the dark woodland floor. Tired of a materialistic, warring world, Arp and other Dadaists sought in such works a new "mystical reality."

Jean Arp: *Forest,* 1916

Mustache Hat

The Sea

A Navel

Mustache Watch

The Navel Bottle

Arabian Eight

Eggbeater

The seven drawings above show how Dadaist
Jean Arp took the most commonplace
components—hats, navels, bottles,
mustaches—and imaginatively reduced them
to provocative free-form designs.

work and discuss the newest currents in art. Early in 1916, he talked a
retired Dutch sailor named Ephraim Jan into renting him a large room
in the Meierei (Dairy) Inn at No. 1 Spiegelgasse, a narrow street in the
old quarter of town. The Cabaret Voltaire, as Ball and his wife, Emmy
Hennings, called their venture, opened on February 5. "Our cabaret is
a gesture," Ball wrote in his diary. "Every word spoken or sung here
says at least one thing, that these humiliating times have not succeeded in wresting respect from us."

The first evenings at the Cabaret Voltaire were relatively mild affairs.
Ball played the piano, and Emmy Hennings sang songs in French and
Danish. Tristan Tzara, a pale, nervous little Romanian poet with bris-
tling dark hair and intelligent eyes behind thick glasses, recited verses
in his native tongue. A balalaika band played Russian folk songs. The
décor had been provided partly by Tzara's tall fellow countryman,
Marcel Janco, who had made some large and rather terrifying masks
that he painted blood red, and partly by an Alsatian painter named Jean
Arp (he had been christened Hans but came to prefer Jean), who contributed paintings by himself and by a few of the artists he had known
in Paris, including Pablo Picasso. Arp had been living in Paris before
the War, and he was on friendly terms with Picasso, Delaunay and
other leading Cubists. His mixed citizenship—his mother was German,
his father French—convinced him that "the War was no good for me,"
and in 1915, when it looked as though he would be forced to join the
French Army, he had sought refuge in neutral Switzerland. There he
was notified by the German consul that the Reich considered him a
German subject—Strasbourg, his birthplace, belonged to Germany
then—and therefore subject to deportation and conscription into the
German Army. At the preliminary examination in Zurich, he was asked
to fill out a form containing about 30 questions, the first of which referred to his date of birth. Arp wrote the date—16/9/87—in the space
provided, put down the same figure in answer to all the other questions, and then drew a line at the bottom of the page and added up the
entries. Solemnly removing all his clothes, he handed the form to a
startled official, who urged him to get dressed and go home. Arp was
not bothered again.

The little Cabaret Voltaire, which could accommodate about 50 people at a time, was immediately popular with students and well-to-do
Swiss burghers. Success emboldened the collaborators. Their nightly
performances soon took on an increasingly aggressive character, as
they made use of shock tactics to express their contempt for a world
gone mad. Tzara, Janco and Richard Huelsenbeck, a young German
poet, medical student and political agitator who had recently come
from Berlin, initiated the practice of simultaneous readings—an idea
borrowed from the Italian Futurists who used to create an effect of
utter chaos by reciting different poems simultaneously. Weird dances,
including a number called "*Noir Cacadou*" that featured Huelsenbeck
and Tzara with their heads encased in stovepipes, were accompanied by
the sound of someone banging on a tin can or yapping like a dog (noise
music, or *bruitisme*, was another Futurist technique). Janco fabricated

costumes out of paper, cardboard and colored rags, and everyone participated in the action.

In addition to this nightly tumult, the collaborators also managed to write poems, paint pictures and put out an international review called *Cabaret Voltaire*, whose first issue included writings by Apollinaire, Tzara, Huelsenbeck, Marinetti and Blaise Cendrars, and reproductions of drawings by Picasso, Modigliani, Arp, Kandinsky, Otto van Rees and Janco. This first issue also placed in print for the first time the word that the little group in Zurich had chosen to give to their various activities. A dispute still simmers as to just who found the famous word and under what circumstances. All that can be said with assurance is that while going through a French-German dictionary at random, someone in the original group came upon the French word *dada*, a child's word for a hobbyhorse, and that the others immediately accepted it. "It's just made for our purpose," Huelsenbeck said (or says he said). "The child's first sound expresses the primitiveness, the beginning at zero, the new in our art. We could not find a better word."

The two-syllable nonsense term became a battle cry with which the Dadaists drove themselves and their audiences to ever-greater frenzies of excitement. They soon started putting on performances in various halls around Zurich—"Dada Nights" made up of wild "Cubist" dances, shouted simultaneous recitations, noise music, "static poems" (a Tzara invention that consisted of hanging large printed cards on chairs and changing them at intervals), and obscenities hurled at the audience, which sometimes flung back insults of a more material kind. The first Dada texts appeared in the summer of 1916: Huelsenbeck's *Phantastische Gebete (Fantastic Prayers)*, a collection of nonsense verses ("indigo indigo/streetcar sleeping-bag/bedbug and flea/indigo indigai/ umbaliska/bumm Dadai") with woodcut illustrations by Arp, and Tzara's *La Première Aventure Céleste de M. Antipyrine (The First Celestial Adventure of Mr. Antipyrine)*, described by Tzara as "a boxing match with words." In March of 1917 the center of operations was shifted to the Galerie Dada, a larger hall where the Dadaists performed and exhibited their work and the work of other artists such as Kandinsky and Paul Klee, while insisting more and more strenuously that, in Tzara's words, "art is not serious I assure you" and that Dada was "definitely against the future." They also showed paintings by Hans Richter, a new recruit who, together with the Swedish painter Viking Eggeling, would later pioneer the use of motion picture film as an art medium.

Although several of the early Dadaists were artists, Dada itself was never an art movement. It was first and foremost a revolutionary state of mind, a violent assault on all accepted values. "All of us were enemies of the old rationalistic, bourgeois art which we regarded as symptomatic of a culture about to crumble with the War," Huelsenbeck wrote. "We loathed every form of an art that merely imitated nature and we admired, instead, the Cubists and Picasso." But if no Dada school of art ever existed, Dada nevertheless served to crystallize a number of attitudes and ideas that had been gaining ground for some time, and which have become very prominent in our own time. The

The Dada movement was accompanied
by a rash of small magazines which argued
the cause of anti-art. Alfred Stieglitz,
a pioneer of creative photography,
published *291*; Francis Picabia, a frequent
contributor, portrayed Stieglitz
as a camera on the cover of one issue.

Few Dada magazines lasted more than one
issue, but *Dada*, the sturdy product of
Tristan Tzara's editorship, proved an
exception and continued for three years.
Its typography, layout and philosophy
defiantly violated all the conventions
of good taste in publishing.

most important of these was that art should no longer be an *interpretation* of reality: it should become, instead, a piece of reality itself.

This notion can be seen clearly in the development of Arp, who was by far the most gifted artist of the original Cabaret Voltaire group. Until about 1915, Arp had been painting canvases that showed the influence of Cubism and Futurism; few of these exist today, for he managed to destroy almost all of his pre-Dada work. In Zurich, Arp and his companion Sophie Taeuber, a young dancer and art teacher whom he married in 1922, began experimenting with various "non-art" materials to make works that appeared themselves like bits of reality. "Sophie Taeuber and I," he wrote later, "had decided to renounce completely the use of oil colors in our compositions. We wanted to avoid any reminder of the paintings which seemed to us to be characteristic of a pretentious, self-satisfied world." They worked together on large collages of cloth and paper, in which the placement of dark and light forms was arrived at by the laws of chance—letting the cutout forms fall freely upon the surface. "Intuition led me to revere the law of chance as the highest and deepest of laws," he wrote, "the law that rises from the fundament." At first, when these fragile collages began to deteriorate, Arp made strenuous efforts to repair them. Gradually, though, he began to feel the need to incorporate in his work the factor of change, death and metamorphosis that was always present in nature. Walking in the woods or on the shores of the Swiss lakes, he and Sophie would gather stones or bits of wood which he would bring home and sketch over and over again, refining and simplifying the natural shapes in an effort to extract the essential form that would express both continuity and change, being and becoming. The egglike but asymmetrical ovals and other shapes, which appeared first in his carved wood *Reliefs* of 1916 and 1917, were to become Arp's permanent "symbols of metamorphosis and the future of human bodies."

Arp may well have been the least Dadaistic of the early Dadaists. His gentle, quiet nature did not lend itself to violent assaults on the public taste, and his humor, which expressed itself in some delightfully odd poetry, lacked the harsh bite of Dada. Most of the Dadaists were essentially rather humorless, and their wildest jokes often seemed to hover between idealism and despair. In Zurich, Arp recalled years later, "We spoke of Dada as of a crusade that would win back the promised land of the Creative." It was in his Dada period that Arp found his true direction as an artist, however, and in doing so he illuminated the constructive force of a movement that has so often been described as being wholly anti-art. "The important thing about Dada," he once wrote, ". . . is that the Dadaists despised what is commonly regarded as art, but put the whole universe on the lofty throne of art. We declared that everything that comes into being or is made by man is art."

Nothing exemplifies Arp's statement better than the readymades of Marcel Duchamp, although in 1916 the Dadaists in Zurich and the avant-garde circle in New York were unaware of each other. Contact came about largely through the frail little magazines put out by both groups. While the Dadaists sought to transmit their ideas and broaden their attack through the publication of a review that they had renamed *DADA* (its first number appeared in July 1917), Duchamp continued his quiet undermining of high art in two issues of *The Blind Man* and a single issue of *Rongwrong* (the spelling of the title was a printer's error that Duchamp retained). Stieglitz's review *291* was languishing when Picabia went to Barcelona for three months in 1916, rallied a group of refugee artists there, and put out four issues of a magazine that he called, with Stieglitz's permission, *391*. This journal was dominated by Picabia's eccentric typography and his witty, machine-style drawings, but it also printed illustrations by others.

The most colorful member of the Barcelona group was Arthur Cravan, a natural Dadaist who claimed to be a nephew of Oscar Wilde. Cravan wrote poetry of a sort but was better known for his savage printed attacks on almost every writer or painter of any consequence. A giant of a man, he was also a professional prize fighter and he had recently gone into the ring in Barcelona with the Negro world heavyweight champion, Jack Johnson, who knocked him out in the first round—a minor exercise for Johnson, since Cravan had prepared for the fray by getting himself roaring drunk.

Momentarily enriched by this fiasco, Cravan left Barcelona early in 1917 and came to New York, where Duchamp and Picabia, who had recently returned, arranged for him to give a lecture on modern art at the Grand Central Gallery. They hoped to create a scandal, and they were not disappointed. A large audience, which included many wealthy and socially prominent ladies eager for esthetic enlightenment, waited for an hour or more until Cravan made his unsteady appearance and tottered up to the platform. He took off his jacket, muttering incoherently and waving his arms about in such a way as to endanger a large painting by the academic American artist Alfred Sterner, which was hanging directly behind him. Then he began to remove his pants. In the midst of this process he leaned forward on the lectern and started to shout insults and obscenities at the audience. The police, who had already been summoned, rushed out at this point and subdued him, and only some fast and persuasive argument by Walter Arensberg prevented his being thrown into jail.

With America's entry into the War on April 6, 1917, the atmosphere in New York became decreasingly favorable to scandal and subversion—even artistic subversion. Picabia, restless as always, left for Paris in the fall. Although he was often drunk and suffering from a nervous disorder, he continued to put out *391*. Early in 1918, his wife persuaded him to consult a famous neurologist in Lausanne, and while he was there Picabia made contact with the Dada group in Zurich.

The meeting set off a great burst of Dada energy. "Long live Picabia, the antipainter arrived from New York!" proclaimed Tzara in *DADA 3*, and he went on to laud the newcomer for having brought about "the annihilation of traditional beauty." This issue's wild typographical eccentricity was in sharp contrast to the generally neat appearance of the previous numbers, and it added immeasurably to the discomforts of Jules Heuberger, the harassed Zurich printer who put out the

Dadaist magazines also cropped up in Germany. An early issue of *Der Dada*, a publication founded by editor Raoul Hausmann in Berlin, displayed eccentric typography, vignetted illustrations from dictionaries, proofreader's marks, a woodcut and the statement that "He who eats of Dada dies if he is not Dada."

In 1920 Richard Huelsenbeck published *Dada Almanach*, the last important Dadaist magazine. In it were poems on Dada's birth, a history of the Zurich movement, and an attack on abstract painting. On the cover was a cross-eyed head of Beethoven.

Dadaist tracts between jail sentences for publishing anarchist leaflets.

The War was ending, and Dada, whose two separate strains had now merged, was about to enter a new and sensational phase. Tzara's 1918 manifesto, which he read from the stage of Meisen Hall in Zurich on March 23, sounded the apocalyptic note:

> . . . I say unto you: there is no beginning and we do not tremble, we are not sentimental. We are a furious wind, tearing the dirty linen of clouds and prayers, preparing the great spectacle of disaster, fire, decomposition. . . .
> Let each man proclaim: there is a great negative work of destruction to be accomplished. We must sweep and clean. Affirm the cleanliness of the individual after the state of madness, aggressive complete madness of a world abandoned to the hands of bandits, who rend one another and destroy the centuries. . . .
> Dada; abolition of logic, which is the dance of those impotent to create: . . . Dada; abolition of memory: Dada; abolition of archeology: Dada; abolition of prophets: Dada; abolition of the future: Dada; absolute and unquestionable faith in every god that is the immediate product of spontaneity. . . . Freedom: Dada Dada Dada, a roaring of tense colors, and interlacing of opposites and of all contradictions, grotesques, inconsistencies: LIFE.

Sired by a profound disgust with the War and all the so-called rationalism of a society that had produced it, Dadaism would soon erupt in most of the world's great cities, but it inevitably found its true postwar headquarters in the ancient home of rationalism, Paris. In 1919 Picabia returned to Paris, where he continued to put out *391* and kept in close touch with the Dada group in Zurich. He was soon joined by Duchamp, who had spent the previous nine months in Buenos Aires. Much had changed in their absence. Apollinaire, the spokesman for the new movement, was dead; weakened by a severe head wound in the War, he had succumbed to the influenza epidemic of 1918. A number of other artists had been victims of the War, including the prodigiously gifted Raymond Duchamp-Villon, Duchamp's brother. Picabia and Duchamp soon made contact with a group of young Frenchmen, poets for the most part, who had seen at first hand the grotesque savagery of modern war and who were immediately receptive to the sweeping antilogic of Dadaism. These young men—André Breton, Louis Aragon, Philippe Soupault and Paul Eluard—all contributed to the Zurich review *DADA*, and they published the work of the Zurich Dadaists in their own journal, *Littérature* (the magazine's title was a mockery, since these men were attempting to create an antiliterature analogous to Picabia's and Duchamp's anti-ärt productions).

During the first week of January 1920, Tristan Tzara arrived in Paris and was put up on a sofa in Picabia's apartment in the Rue Emile-Augier. Tzara's genius for publicity and calculated outrage was as effective in Paris as it had been in Zurich: it soon proved to be the spark that lit the Dada fuse. The first public demonstration of Dada in Paris took place at the Palais des Fêtes on January 23, sponsored by the review *Littérature*. A large audience had gathered to observe the antics of these bizarre young people who were causing such a stir. They heard Breton, Aragon and Georges Ribemont-Dessaignes (a friend of Picabia's) read their incomprehensible poems—some of them simultaneously—and were then subjected to Tzara's reading of a "poem" that was actually an article from the day's newspaper, but which was drowned out by the loud bells and buzzers that sounded continuously through the reading. The audience, thoroughly exasperated, shouted its disapproval. The Dadaists immediately began planning bigger and more provocative demonstrations.

One of Tzara's favorite tricks in Zurich had been to feed the press false information of all kinds about the Dadaists. He now let it be known that Charlie Chaplin would deliver a lecture on Dada at the Salon des Indépendants, on February 5. An even larger audience turned out this time, and, infuriated to learn that the Chaplin announcement was a Dada trick, kept up a steady roar of indignation while the Dadaists read their manifestoes from the stage.

Overnight, it seemed, Dada had become a *cause célèbre*. Attacked in the conservative press as a dangerous menace, of German or perhaps even Bolshevik origin, it was defended by such prominent intellectuals as André Gide, whom the Dadaists thereupon rewarded with a shower of insults: "If you read André Gide aloud for ten minutes, your breath will stink," Picabia announced. The Cubist painters formally dissociated themselves from the Dadaists, who were only too happy to sever their ties with art. Picabia kept the pot boiling in the pages of *391*. The cover for the sensational March number was a reproduction of a new and exceptionally provocative Duchamp readymade—a photograph of the Mona Lisa that Duchamp had "assisted" by adding a mustache and goatee. Inside could be found Picabia's "portrait" of *The Holy Virgin*, which was a full-page splatter of ink.

Duchamp had gone back to New York by this time, but his anti-art spirit seemed to preside over the Dada ferment. The fact that Duchamp took no part in the Dadaist demonstrations only seemed to enhance his reputation. When the Dada exhibition at the Galerie Montaigne in the spring of 1920 was being planned, the organizers wired Duchamp in New York, requesting several of his works; Duchamp wired back a rather vulgar pun meaning, roughly, "Nuts to you," and the exhibitors hung his telegram instead.

The 1920 Dada season reached a climax with a chaotic performance on May 26 at the Salle Gaveau, a famous old concert hall generally associated with recitals of chamber music. Whereas the earlier performances had been largely improvised, an effort was made this time to produce an especially powerful effect. The Dadaists had announced that they would all have their heads shaved on stage. Instead, they presented a series of idiotic skits by Soupault, Breton and Ribemont-Dessaignes, and Tzara's new nonsense "play" *La Deuxième Aventure de Monsieur Aa, l'Antipyrine*. The audience had used the intermission to go out and buy a quantity of produce from the local market, and its members came back prepared to vent their feelings. "For the first time

Duchamp made an "assisted readymade" of the *Mona Lisa (detail, above)* when he added a mustache and goatee to a reproduction of the Leonardo masterpiece, dramatizing his personal, and Dadaistic, point of view that art had become too precious and too expensive. Years later he signed an unaltered print of the *Mona Lisa*, subtitling it "*Rasée*"—French for "shaved."

in the history of the world," Tzara wrote proudly, "people threw at us not only eggs, salads and pennies, but beefsteaks as well . . . . The audience were extremely Dadaist."

In a single season, Dada had become too successful for its own good. Being defended by intellectuals like André Gide had been bad enough; now its audiences were entering more and more fully into the Dadaist spirit at each performance, and enjoying themselves thoroughly—a form of acceptance that Dada could not accept. The movement's destructive nature demanded new outrages. André Breton reportedly favored turning it into a secret society that would work to undermine the authority of public figures. Breton took the lead the following spring in organizing the mock "trial" of Maurice Barrès, a well-known French writer who had abandoned his youthful liberal views to become a militant patriot and a bigot. Both Tzara and Picabia opposed this proceeding, arguing that it sounded too "serious" and that it would look as though Dada were embracing liberal causes instead of attacking every cause impartially. Breton prevailed, however, and the "trial" took place on Friday, May 13, 1921, in the Hall of Learned Societies, before a predominantly student audience. Barrès, tried in absentia, was subjected to every sort of calumny by the Dadaist tribunal (Breton, naturally, was the judge). When the "Unknown Soldier" appeared in a filthy German uniform and began to bellow abuse at patriotism in every form, several students in the audience leaped up to attack him bodily, and the performance disintegrated into a melee.

The next spring, Breton tried to organize a great international congress of intellectuals and artists of every stripe to discuss the principles of modernism in the arts. This hardly seemed the sort of destructive activity that Dada was supposed to favor, and Tzara, among others, flatly refused to go along with the idea. Breton thereupon published an extremely violent attack on Tzara, whom he described in the journal *Comoedia* as "an impostor avid of publicity." His intemperate language got him into trouble with the other members of the organizing committee for what had come to be called the Congress of Paris, and the whole matter ended with a kind of trial of Breton at the Closerie des Lilas, a famous old Montparnasse restaurant frequented by artists and literary men. The meeting was attended by all the leading members of the Paris intelligentsia, including Picasso, Matisse, Brancusi, Jean Cocteau and even Erik Satie.

The American writer Matthew Josephson has described the scene in his autobiographical *Life among the Surrealists.* "Never in my experience were words of such passion and flame hurled at each other by men without coming to blows," Josephson wrote. "Breton spoke in rolling periods in his own defense, while Tzara, leaping to the attack, fairly screamed in his high voice, talking so fast that I could not follow him. Erik Satie, the comic spirit of modern music, a paunchy man with gold-rimmed pince-nez and a goatee, presided as 'judge' and seemed to be laughing over the affair. . . . In the end—after all sorts of absurd charges had been hurled back and forth—the consensus of the meeting was expressed in a vote of nonconfidence in Breton and his proposed

Congress of Paris—which thus, in its preparatory stages, collapsed."

The collapse of Dadaism in Paris followed soon afterward. Breton haughtily withdrew, announcing that Dadaism had been merely "a state of mind which served to keep us in a state of readiness—from which we shall now start out, in all lucidity, toward that which calls us." (Two years later he would identify the new movement: Surrealism.) Picabia, who had been bored with Dada for some time, amused himself by attacking all the Dadaists in one-shot publications like *La Pomme de Pins (The Pine Cone)*. Tzara replied with polemics of his own, and continued to stage occasional demonstrations that kept the movement alive for another year or so. But Tzara himself had said that "the true dadas are against Dada," and it was becoming increasingly evident that Dada's anarchic energy had been turned in upon itself. By 1924, most of the original Paris Dadaists (not including Tzara) had followed Breton into Surrealism, the new "revolution of consciousness."

In Germany, where Dada took a different course, its active life was just as brief. Richard Huelsenbeck had left Zurich early in 1917 and returned to Berlin, where famine, despair and his own wish "to make literature with a gun in hand" caused Dada to assume a strongly political form. Huelsenbeck had no love for his native country—he once wrote that "Germany always becomes the land of poets and thinkers when it begins to be washed up as the land of judges and butchers." At this stage he saw the Communist Party as Dada's natural ally against German militarism and middle-class stupidity, targets that he himself attacked vigorously in the review *Der Dada* (which also printed the savage drawings of George Grosz), in revolutionary lectures and harangues that were often broken up by the police, and in the climactic Berlin Dada exhibition of 1920, whose central feature was a tailor's dummy with a pig's head, suspended from the ceiling and clad in the uniform of a German officer.

The other center of German Dadaism was Cologne. Jean Arp went to Cologne in 1919 and joined forces there with Max Ernst, a young painter he had known before the War, and Johannes Baargeld, a painter, poet and political activist who founded the Communist Party in the Rhineland. Ernst and Arp collaborated on a series of collages made by cutting images from books and magazines and then altering and reassembling them to create disturbing new apparitions that they called "Fatagaga"—a Dadaist abbreviation for *Fabrication de tableaux garantis gazométriques* (Manufacture of pictures guaranteed to be gasometric). With Baargeld, they also put on one of the most famous exhibitions in the annals of Dada. It was held in a glassed-in courtyard behind a café, which could only be reached through a public urinal. Inside, paying visitors saw Fatagaga and other drawings on the walls; an aquarium filled with red liquid, with a woman's head of hair floating on top and an arm protruding from below the surface; a wooden sculpture to which Ernst had chained a hatchet in case anyone wished to destroy it; and a young girl (live) in a white communion dress who recited obscene poetry. In no time at all someone smashed the aquarium, and the floor was awash with red water. A complaint was lodged with the police, who came to close down the exhibition on grounds of obscenity; on finding, however, that the item that had caused the most indignation was an etching by Albrecht Dürer, they permitted it to stay open.

Ernst left for Paris in 1922. Arp had previously returned to Zurich. Huelsenbeck, disillusioned by the Russian Communists' hostility to modern art, abandoned the revolutionary struggle and embarked on a trip around the world. German Dada was finished, although the Dada spirit would live on for years in the work of an extraordinary natural Dadaist named Kurt Schwitters. A poet as well as a painter, Schwitters, who lived in Hanover, had contributed to the early Dadaist reviews, and since 1919 he had been making collages out of newspaper, buttons, bus tickets, rags, wires and other discarded scraps that he picked up—an activity that was distinctly Dadaist in its substitution of "raw life" for the traditional materials of art. "Every artist must be allowed to mold a picture out of nothing but blotting paper," he once wrote, "provided he is capable of molding a picture." As the latter part of this statement indicates, Schwitters' rubbish art transcends Dada; in his subtle and exquisitely balanced collages, which have profoundly influenced the art of our own time, the refuse of a ruined world was organized into compositions of great beauty, and these may well have struck other Dadaists as being too obviously esthetic.

In any case, Huelsenbeck and his Berlin colleagues considered Schwitters' political attitude hopelessly bourgeois, and they refused to show his work in the 1920 Dada exhibition in Berlin. Schwitters thereupon formulated his own version of Dada, which he called "Merz," a nonsense word that had appeared on a scrap of newspaper in one of his own early collages—it was actually the second syllable of the German word *Kommerz*. Said Schwitters: " 'Merz' stands for freedom from all fetters, for the sake of artistic creation." Working outside the mainstream of Dada, he continued after the movement's demise to fabricate his Merz collages, write his Merz poems in the manner of Gertrude Stein (the most famous is his charming *Anna Blossom Has Wheels*), and give Dadaistic readings and lectures. At one of these public appearances he "read" a poem that consisted of a single letter, W. It began with a whisper, rose slowly to the sound of a wailing siren and ended in a series of short, loud barks. He also invented a "bird language," and visitors to his house in Hanover sometimes found him sitting in a tree in the garden, twittering down at them pleasantly.

Schwitters turned his own house into a Merz sculpture, a fantastic labyrinth of jutting partitions, tunnels and excrescences which he kept on multiplying endlessly until he left Germany for good in 1937. The "Merzbau," which he considered his lifework, was destroyed by Allied bombs during World War II. Schwitters had started work on a new Merzbau in England, under a grant from New York's Museum of Modern Art, when he died in 1948.

What did Dada accomplish in its brief and riotous career? The enormous contemporary interest in the movement—there is today a Dada Association in Paris that puts out a report twice a year—suggests that something more was at issue here than zany behavior and attempts to jolt the bourgeoisie. There is no question that Dada succeeded magnificently in carrying out its "great negative work of destruction," that it shattered the last remnants of an already crumbling body of esthetic tradition and opened the way to the contemporary doctrine of unrestrained creative freedom for the artist. It can be argued that this was not an unmixed blessing; unrestrained creative freedom leads all too often to the worship of novelty for its own sake and encourages the "anything goes" attitude that has made the present period a field day for the charlatan. But few contemporary artists of any stature would deny that Dada forced them to question the basic assumptions of all art and thus cleared the air for fresh and vital experiments. Destruction, as the revolutionary Mikhail Bakunin once said, is also creation.

We may tend at this period to overrate Dada's specific contributions. European art between the two Wars concerned itself primarily, after all, with the old esthetic problems of form and space, and even Surrealism, which arose from the ashes of Dada, was guided by some rather rigid theories about the unconscious—theories that had little to do with the bumptious antilogic of the Dadaists. At another level, though, it has become increasingly clear that Dada embodied in concrete and dramatic form one of the most characteristic problems of art in our time—the true relation between art and life.

In refusing to take an esthetic attitude toward life, the Dadaists were the first to confront this problem directly. "Art is not the most precious manifestation of life," Tristan Tzara wrote in his 1922 *Lecture on Dada*. "Art has not the celestial and universal value that people like to attribute to it. Life is far more interesting. Dada knows the correct measure that should be given to art: with subtle, perfidious methods, Dada introduces it into daily life. And vice versa." Turning their backs on high art, with its artificial ordering of experience and its rational hierarchies of meaning, they opted for "obvious, undifferentiated, unintellectual life," which they saw as a series of irrational collisions ruled by chance, and considered all the more precious because it was being extinguished with such mechanical efficiency on the battlefields.

Life, absurd as it might be, was what mattered. The same idea lies at the heart of much contemporary art and literature, and it is one of the basic principles of Existentialism, the most influential 20th Century philosophy, which postulates individual human action as the sole proof of existence in an absurd universe. This is what Jean-Paul Sartre had in mind when he said, pontifically, "I am the new Dada."

Most of the leading Dadaists went on to become what they had fought so hard against—creative artists like Arp, Ernst and Schwitters, poets like Breton and Tzara and Aragon. Hugo Ball, who founded the Cabaret Voltaire, stayed on in Switzerland and eventually became a religious mystic who was venerated as a kind of saint by the people of his region. Huelsenbeck completed his medical studies and became a practicing psychiatrist in New York. Picabia withdrew into scornful silence, living in partial retirement at Cap d'Antibes. Only Marcel Duchamp, who had remained more or less aloof from the movement, would carry the implications of Dadaism to their logical conclusion.

The Dada Invasion

Dada, the most aggressively radical movement in art history, was born in a tiny café in Zurich, Switzerland, a neutral island in the bloody quagmire of World War I. More than just a reaction against war and the society that fostered it, Dada attacked anything conventional and sacrosanct—government, literature, art. It was, according to Marcel Duchamp, "a sort of nihilism . . . a way to get out of a state of mind—to avoid being influenced by one's immediate environment or by the past, to get away from clichés—to get free."

The Dada spirit coalesced into a tangible movement in 1916 around a volatile group of freethinking intellectuals and artists who wanted to reject the complacent past and protest the horrible present by creating their own world of satire and shocking polemic. The Zurich Dadaists' outcries against a society they found intolerable attracted followers in Berlin, Cologne, Paris and Hanover. And though the movement burned itself out within six years, doomed by the very individuality of its members, its spirit and its innovations still live. In 1966 a navel-shaped plaque *(above)* designed by Dadaist Jean Arp was erected to commemorate the golden anniversary of Dada's birth at the Cabaret Voltaire in Zurich's Spiegelgasse *(right)*. The forces of artistic freedom that Dada unleashed went on to inspire Surrealism, Abstract Expressionism, Pop Art and whatever other strange and new forms art may assume in the future.

This fish-eye photograph of the Spiegelgasse today echoes the symbolism of the navels (painted on the street) which represent Dada's birth and fresh approach. The Café Meierei occupies the site where the Cabaret Voltaire stood.

Hugo Ball in the Cabaret Voltaire, 1916

Emmy Hennings with puppet, 1916

Jean Arp, Tristan Tzara and Hans Richter, 1917

T he normally constituted bourgeois," wrote Jean Arp, "possesses rather less imagination than a worm and has, in place of a heart, a larger-than-life-sized corn which troubles him when there is a change in the weather—the stock exchange weather." Such unbridled contempt for the moneyed middle class and all it held dear was the secret of Dada's meteoric rise to fame in a disillusioned generation.

The first of the arts to come under Dada's attack was poetry; the assault was launched by Hugo Ball, himself a poet in the Dada manner. The gangling conscientious objector once wrote about an early performance at the Cabaret Voltaire, when he recited his works dressed in a Cubist costume *(top, left):* "My legs were encased in a tight-fitting cylindrical pillar of shiny blue cardboard . . . so that I looked like an obelisk. Above this I wore a huge cardboard coat collar, scarlet inside and gold outside, which was fastened at the neck in such a way that I could flap it like a pair of wings by moving my elbows. . . . Everyone was very curious. So, as an obelisk cannot walk, I had myself carried to the platform in a blackout." He then began to recite one of his "sound poems," slowly and majestically: "gadji beri bimba glandridi laula lonni cadori. . . ." Ball's own invention, the "sound poem" was intended "to surrender the word, conserving for poetry its most sacred domain." The wild and brilliant Romanian poet Tristan Tzara wrote a work entitled *Roar:* it consisted of this single word repeated 147 times.

Emmy Hennings, Ball's mistress, sang folk songs and also recited poetry in a shrill voice that irritated audiences as much as the antics of her male colleagues.

Fifty years later, during the 1966 anniversary celebration for Dada, the citizenry of Zurich tried to re-create the electric atmosphere of the Cabaret Voltaire. Inside an elegant café *(bottom, left),* performers read poetry; one even imitated Ball's costume. Outside, a brass band played off-key, children were hired to throw snowballs, and a crowd of 1,000 chanted "Dada is all. Long live Dada." Even the mayor joined in the fun. There was no doubt about it: Dada had come full cycle; it had itself become a bourgeois institution. And this was quite in the Dada spirit: as one Dadaist put it, "The aim of Dada is the destruction of Dada."

Celebration of Dada's 50th Anniversary, Café Odéon, Zurich, February 1966

Jean Arp in his studio, Meudon, 1958

Invention was the essence of Dada art, and two of the most inventive Dadaists in Zurich were Jean Arp *(above)* and his collaborator and wife-to-be Sophie Taeuber. Arp was described by Alfred Barr of The Museum of Modern Art as "a one-man laboratory for the discovery of new form"—such as his egg-smooth sculptures, which have been compared to "clouds on the verge of forming recognizable objects." His ambition was "to teach man what he had forgotten—to dream with his eyes open." Sophie also experimented with abstract drawings and

colorful tapestries such as *Elementary Forms (top, right)*.

Marcel Janco, the Romanian architectural student, cut a dashing figure in his pinstripe suit and cravat. But he was far from formal in his choice of materials—plaster, burlap and masonite form the work at right—and his opinions on art were pure Dada. "Who on earth, in those days of collapse," he later wrote, "was still ready to believe in 'eternal values,' in the 'canned goods' of the past, in the academies, the schools of art? The cry of Dada became universal—to hell with beauty!"

70

Sophie Taeuber-Arp: *Elementary Forms*, 1917

Marcel Janco: *Composition with Red Arrow*, 1919-1920

Francis Picabia: *Very Rare Picture upon the Earth*, 1915

Francis Picabia: *Girl Born without Mother*, 1917

Francis Picabia: *Machine Turns Fast*, 1916-1917

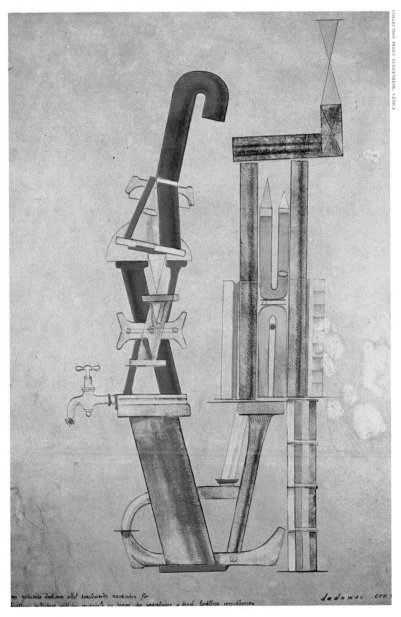

To many of the Dadaists, mechanization threatened to turn men into robots. Francis Picabia satirized this danger in *Very Rare Picture upon the Earth (left)*. Executed in New York a year before Dada's birth in Zurich, it actually has machinelike parts— three-dimensional wooden forms painted with gilt and silver. Like Duchamp's *Large Glass*, Picabia's creations often illustrate mechanized sex: the numbered gears in *Machine Turns Fast (above)* are labeled "man" and "woman." *Girl Born without Mother (above, right)* is not only a poke at sex but may allude to Erichthonius, the "child born without mother," described by Ovid.

Max Ernst, who helped found Dada in Cologne, produced a sex machine carefully drawn in pencil and colored crayons. Childishly innocent at first glance, it reveals on closer examination its humorous overtones. Its inscription begins: "By minimax dadamax, a small machine which he constructed for fearless pollination. . . ."

Max Ernst: *Small Machine Constructed by Minimax Dadamax in Person*, 1919

Kurt Schwitters: The first *Merzbau*, 1923

Kurt Schwitters: *The Lunatic-Doctor*, 1919

74

Kurt Schwitters: Third *Merzbau*, 1948

Of all the Dadaists, only the German Kurt Schwitters was not a professed anti-artist; in fact, he was "absolutely, unreservedly, 24-hours-a-day PRO art," according to the Dada artist and historian Hans Richter. Anything that had been discarded as useless Schwitters eagerly exhumed "and restored to an honored place in life by means of his art," said Richter. His passion for enshrining the refuse of a war-torn civilization culminated in "the cathedral of misery," or *Merzbau (left)*, the showplace of *Merz*, his own brand of Dada. During the War the *Merzbau* was destroyed. He built another museum of *Merz* in Norway. It, too, was demolished. He fled to England and worked until his death in 1948 creating the third *Merzbau (below)*, an immense collage on a barn wall. Its plaster grip holds a watering-can spout, wheel rims and a rubber ball.

Dada's bitterness and pessimism were buried with the movement, but its optimism remained very much alive, largely because of Schwitters. One of his statements epitomizes Dada's most far-reaching contribution. Asked "What is art?" Schwitters replied, "What isn't?"

Tu m', 1918. Detail, below

IV

A Legend
under Glass

What is left of Dada? . . . above all the remarkable personality of Marcel Duchamp, whose spirit, whose moral austerity and haughty detachment, whose experiments and profound thought surpassed the limits of Dada.
—GEORGES HUGNET

It could perhaps be argued that Duchamp was never a true Dadaist. Dadaism's anti-art violence really proclaimed the vitality of art, in the same way that the passionate atheist, by the very force of his denial, affirms the power of religion. As Duchamp himself once pointed out, the only way to be truly anti-art is to be indifferent to it, and from the time of his first trip to New York in 1915, he had shown an increasing indifference to any of the recognized forms of art. Why, then, did he choose to remain within the art world at all? Why not turn his back on it entirely, as Rimbaud did? The question, like so many others about Duchamp, remains unanswered.

He painted one new picture in 1918, his first in four years. Katherine S. Dreier, a formidable persuader, had asked him for a painting to fit the long, narrow space over the library door in her apartment on Central Park West in New York. Duchamp's canvas, entitled *Tu m'*, became a sort of inventory of his principal ideas and preoccupations up to that time. The composition *(page 76)* is dominated by three readymades—bicycle wheel, corkscrew, hat rack—whose shadows he projected on the surface and then traced by rubbing a lead pencil over them. The sinuous contours of the *Standard Stoppages*, his "new forms to the unit of length" obtained by dropping three one-meter threads from a height of one meter, appear at bottom left and again to the right of the picture. A long row of overlapping squares of color, suggesting paint samples and executed with mathematical precision, runs the gamut from gray to yellow and leads the eye to what looks like a large rent in the canvas, from which protrudes a bottle brush; the rent is an illusion, painted in *trompe l'oeil*, but the bottle brush is real and so are the three safety pins used to "close" the illusory rent. Just beneath this double deception is a pointing hand that was executed by a professional sign painter whom Duchamp hired for this purpose and whose signature, "A. Klang," is visible below. The bright color (unusual for Duchamp since his Fauve period) and the delicate balance of the composition make this one of Duchamp's more superficially pleasing paintings. Duchamp always considered it a mere résumé. His somewhat mystifying title for it, *Tu m'*, is generally believed to be an

In Duchamp's last painting on canvas, a veritable catalogue of his ideas and techniques, he made visual puns on the artist's craft —color swatches, a bottle brush poked through a painted rip—and traced shadows of some readymades.

abbreviation for the French *tu m'ennuies* (you bore me), which may have expressed his own attitude toward the painting or its recipient or art in general—Duchamp had nothing to say on the matter. In any event, it was to be his last formal painting on canvas. Soon after completing it, he left New York for Buenos Aires. While there, he sent directions to his sister Suzanne in Paris for the construction of an *Unhappy Readymade:* a geometry textbook, to be hung from the balcony of Suzanne's Paris apartment so that the problems and theorems, exposed to the test of wind, sun and rain, could get "the facts of life." Suzanne carried out his instructions faithfully and painted a picture of the result.

Duchamp returned to Paris in 1919. Although his disdain for groups kept him from participating actively in the Dada movement, he met all the Dadaists at Picabia's apartment, where he was staying, or else at their favorite bar, the Café Certa, and his effect on those young rebels who held nothing and no one sacred was mesmerizing. The Dadaist writer Pierre de Massot has described his first meeting with Duchamp, "whom I had been hearing about for more than a year, and whose every act, every word that was repeated to me, had opened up unlimited perspectives on the future. . . . Immediately, I liked that face, that admirable profile of a purity without equal, that sovereign elegance in clothing, gestures and speaking, that kind of haughty dandyism that tempered the most exquisite politeness and that silent laugh that cut the ground from under pedants." Duchamp's maltreatment of the *Mona Lisa* was in its quiet way as savage an attack on traditional art as anything the Dadaists managed to think up, and his payment of a $115 dentist's bill with an elaborately fabricated check drawn on "The Teeth's Loan & Trust Company, Consolidated" *(page 81)* was itself pure Dada. Early in 1920, though, feeling perhaps that his territory was being encroached upon in Paris, Duchamp went back to New York.

I n addition to picking up where he had left off on the *Large Glass,* he became involved with experiments in the fields of motion (which had interested him since 1911) and optics. He discovered, quite by accident, that when two spirals revolve on a common axis but slightly off-center, one appears to come forward and the other to go back—the so-called "corkscrew effect." Duchamp built an apparatus in 1920 to demonstrate this principle. It consisted of five rectangular glass plates of graduated lengths, each one having black lines painted at each end, attached to a metal rod that was turned by a motor. Man Ray, who was then on his way to becoming one of the most original photographers of the time—he had taken up photography as a means of getting good reproductions of his own paintings, but it was becoming a full-time job—brought his camera in to photograph Duchamp's *Revolving Glass* and was nearly decapitated when one of the glass plates shattered while turning at high speed.

The *Revolving Glass* led Duchamp, some five years later, to construct another machine along similar lines, called the *Rotary Demi-Sphere, Precision Optics,* which also incorporated a virtually untranslatable pun. This *Rotative Demi-Sphère, Optique de Précision* (to give it its French name) consisted of a half-globe mounted on a disc covered with black velvet; the globe was painted with white spirals against a black back-

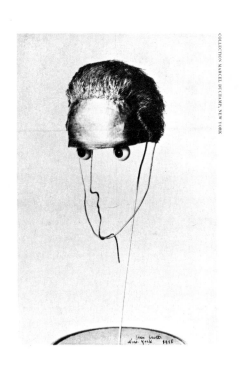

Jean Crotti, an inventive artist who married Duchamp's sister Suzanne, made this striking portrait of his future brother-in-law in lead wire with a carefully modeled pate of fabric and hair and two perfectly colored porcelain eyes. Crotti's experiment with wire constructions, done in 1915, pre-dates by about 10 years similar likenesses by the American sculptor Alexander Calder.

ground. On a copper frame surrounding the disc were the words *"Rrose Sélavy et moi esquivons les ecchymoses des esquimaux aux mots exquis."* Inscription, disc and globe were mounted on a stand and rotated by an electric motor set in the base—the effect, both optical and kinetic, was somewhat like that of a mechanical belly dancer.

The inscription about the *"esquimaux aux mots exquis"* was to appear, in truncated form, in another Duchamp work a year later. Duchamp and Man Ray collaborated on a film in which Duchamp's revolving spirals alternated with his verbal corkscrews, among them the inscription from the *Rotary Demi-Sphere* minus the words *"Rrose Sélavy et moi."* The film's title was suitably Duchampian: *Anemic Cinema.*

Soon after his return to New York, Duchamp felt the need for a change of identity. The fact that he chose a female alter ego, "Rrose Sélavy," and even had himself photographed by Man Ray in a woman's clothes to signalize the event, puzzled a number of his friends and doubtless gave rise to considerable psychoanalytic speculation. Duchamp's own explanation is characteristically free of logic. "It was sort of a readymadeish action," he said. "I first wanted to get a Jewish name, which I thought would be very good in view of my Catholic background. But I didn't find one. Then the idea jumped at me, why not a female name? Marvelous! Much better than to change religion would be to change sex. 'Rose' was just the corniest girl's name at that time in France, and Sélavy, of course, is *c'est la vie.* The two r's in Rrose came about the next year, when Picabia did a painting called *The Cacodylactic Eye* that he wanted all his friends to sign. In signing I wrote the word *arroser*, and the two r's in that gave me the idea of keeping them in the name." Rrose Sélavy soon appeared in a readymade, as the woman of fashion on the label of a perfume called "Belle Haleine—Eau de Voilette" ("Beautiful Breath—Veil Water"), and a photograph of this new work served as the cover for still another Duchamp-edited magazine, called *New York Dada*, whose one and only issue contained, among other items, a manifesto by Tzara and a cartoon by Rube Goldberg.

Rrose also took to coining puns and signing readymades of her own, such as the two that appeared in 1920 and 1921. The first of these, which Duchamp gave to Katherine Dreier, was *Fresh Widow*, a carpenter's window sample (French window) whose panes had been covered with squares of polished black leather (freshly widowed). The second was a small bird cage which is filled with what look like lumps of sugar but are in fact blocks of white marble, and out of which project a thermometer and a cuttlebone; the title of this oddity, which Duchamp presented to Miss Dreier's sister, Dorothea, and which is now on display in the Philadelphia Museum of Art, is *Why Not Sneeze?* All these artifacts perform more or less the same basic function, requiring us to make a verbal and/or visual somersault and thereby creating a "new thought" for a familiar object. They are not so much objects in the physical sense as objects of the mind—"brain facts" *(cervellités)*, as Duchamp once described them.

Significantly, Duchamp's Dadaistic and anti-art activities did not prevent him from playing a vital role in the formation of two of the most important collections of 20th Century art. Ever since 1915, when Du-

Duchamp's features, in the guise of his alter ego, Rrose Sélavy, were reproduced on the label of a perfume bottle which appeared on the cover for *New York Dada*, a one-issue magazine he edited. Rrose Sélavy was also the author of several puns and the two readymades shown on the following page.

Rrose Sélavy made *Fresh Widow* during
Duchamp's visit to New York in 1920 and
1921. The work is an ironic pun utilizing
a carpenter's sample French window with
black leather for panes. *Why Not Sneeze?*
(below) was commissioned by Katherine
Dreier's sister, who refused to accept the
completed object—a bird cage filled with
sugar-cube-sized lumps of marble,
a thermometer and a cuttlebone.

champ first came to New York, Walter Arensberg had sought his advice
on new painters and sculptors, both European and American, and he often
commissioned Duchamp to procure individual works for his growing collection. Duchamp continued to function as Arensberg's unofficial adviser
when he returned from Paris in 1920. That same year, he also consented
to collaborate in a pioneering venture by his old friend and patroness
Katherine Dreier. Miss Dreier had channeled her passion for modern art
into a personal crusade. She had decided to found an educational institution, a society that would put on modern art exhibitions (using her
own collection as a basis), arrange lectures and devote itself to converting
the public—which remained either indifferent or hostile—to the cause
of contemporary art. A domineering woman of tireless energy and Wag-
nerian proportions, she was the antithesis of Duchamp in every possible
way, and they got along famously. It was Man Ray, whom Duchamp had
recommended as vice-president, who gave the organization its title: "Société Anonyme, Inc." As Miss Dreier never tired of explaining, the
term "*société anonyme*" in French was equivalent to the English term
"incorporated," so the name really meant "incorporated corporation." It
was the first institution devoted to modern art in America, preceding by
nine years the founding of the Museum of Modern Art for which, in a
sense, it had prepared the way.

In 1921 during a six months' sojourn in Paris, Duchamp produced a
single new readymade called *La Bagarre d'Austerlitz (The Brawl at Austerlitz)*. Another carpenter's window sample, this one had real glass panes
bearing the glazier's white mark to show that they had just been installed.
The title is a highly complicated pun referring both to the railway station
of Austerlitz in Paris and to the famous Napoleonic battle. In January
1922 he was back in New York again, and working once more on the *Large
Glass*. The work proceeded without undue haste. One phase, in fact, consisted entirely of a process that Duchamp called "dust breeding"—he let
the dust build up for six months on the glass panels in his studio, preparatory to sealing in this accumulation with varnish on the area of the
composition that he referred to as the "sieves"; this was for the purpose
of getting a color that "did not come from the tube." Man Ray photographed the *Glass* with its six months' accumulation of dust, and the
result looked something like a closeup of the moon.

More and more now, the *Glass* was taking on the legendary aura of a
famous work that no one had seen. When Walter Arensberg and his wife,
the original owners, moved permanently to Los Angeles in 1921, they gra-
ciously sold the *Large Glass* to Katherine Dreier so that Duchamp could
continue to work on it. He continued working, in his manner, for another
two years. And then one day in February 1923 he stopped. The *Large
Glass* was far from being finished. Several important elements of the original conception had not even been suggested visually. But after 10 years,
Duchamp was bored with it. *The Bride Stripped Bare by Her Bachelors,
Even*, the most enigmatic and by all odds the most complex work of art
produced in our time, had reached what Duchamp called its "definitive
stage of incompletion."

There is no really satisfactory explanation for the fact that Duchamp failed to complete his great work. But this does not seem to have troubled Duchamp in the least. Even the accidental breaking of the *Glass* itself failed to strike him as especially tragic. In 1926, following an exhibition at the Brooklyn Museum in which it had appeared, the two panels were placed one on top of the other, packed in a wooden carton and loaded rather casually on the bed of a truck for the trip back to Miss Dreier's house in Connecticut. The carton remained closed for several years. When it was finally opened in 1936 and the work inside was discovered to be a mass of splintered fragments, Duchamp calmly set to work repairing it. He worked for three months in Miss Dreier's garage, re-assembling each little shard and splinter and clamping the whole between two heavier sheets of glass. The intricate network of cracks, in which some admirers saw a striking resemblance to the *Standard Stoppages*, neither pleased nor distressed him. We can only conclude that for Duchamp, the visual realization of his ideas was never as important as the ideas themselves. Painting was above all a mental act.

Before venturing into the strange and marvelous country of Duchamp's *Large Glass*, the explorer would be well advised to check his equipment. Good eyesight, a lively imagination and a certain familiarity with the development of modern art, useful though they may be, will prove insufficient in this case because the *Glass* itself, the nine-foot-high object that stands today in the Philadelphia Museum of Art, is only one part of *The Bride Stripped Bare by Her Bachelors, Even*. The other part is to be found in the written notations that Duchamp collected between 1912 and 1923 and finally published in facsimile in 1934 under the title *Boîte Verte (Green Box)*. This is a collection of 93 documents of varying size and shape, describing in elliptical, poetic and often absurd language the purpose and function of every element in the *Glass*.

Duchamp planned originally to have the notes made up into a kind of catalogue "like the Sears, Roebuck catalogue," as he described it, which would then be exhibited together with the *Glass* so that the viewer could consult both simultaneously. He never got around to doing this, but he has often said that he considers the notes at least as important as their visual representation in the *Large Glass*, and some knowledge of the notes is absolutely essential to any understanding of the work as a whole. Fortunately, a translation of the notes by art historian George Heard Hamilton, arranged and put into book form in a typographic facsimile by the British painter Richard Hamilton (no relation to the translator), made this indispensable piece of equipment available to a wider public.

The *Glass* itself is to be viewed not only in its entirety, but in its individual parts which, machinelike, have their own functions within the larger function of the whole. These various segments, furthermore, are logical developments of earlier Duchampian conceptions: the *Large Glass*, therefore, should be looked at in its historical context as well as for its immediate significance. An examination of this kind—a guided tour, so to speak—through Duchamp's strange and fascinating masterpiece is undertaken on the following pages, with descriptive passages that are either derived or directly quoted from the translations of the documents which Duchamp collected in the *Green Box*.

In 1919, in the true Dada spirit, Duchamp made up a fake check which he gave to his dentist in payment of a bill for $115. Drawn on the "Teeth's Loan and Trust Company, Consolidated," the bogus check was accepted by the dentist, who later proved himself equal to the prank by selling the check back to Duchamp for more than its face value.

Through the "Large Glass"

In the 40-odd years since he stopped working on it, Marcel Duchamp's unfinished magnum opus *The Bride Stripped Bare by Her Bachelors, Even* (also known simply as the *Large Glass*) has been all but ignored by the art world; today, however, it is gradually gaining a reputation as one of the most important works of the century. In the cryptic forms and tracings sandwiched between its nine-foot cracked glass panels, critics have professed to see meanings ranging from the frivolous to the Freudian; through it all the *Glass* has remained as enigmatic a challenge as the *Mona Lisa*'s smile.

For this is quintessentially the world of Marcel Duchamp, and it is like no other. It is a work in which visual and verbal concepts hold equal sway: it cannot be deciphered without reference to his notes—many scribbled on scraps of paper—which Duchamp collected in the *Green Box (opposite)*. Because the *Glass* cannot be looked at without being looked *through* at the same time, it tends to absorb into its world everything else visible around or behind it; its own background is thus an ever-changing readymade. And if its individual parts are fascinating, its total effect is unique: this is a vision of the fourth-dimensional world of Duchamp's innermost ideas. The *Large Glass*, in sum, is its own reality and can only be viewed as such—the logic of the everyday has no place here. On the following pages, author Tomkins conducts a guided tour through Duchamp's masterwork.

Companion-piece to the *Large Glass*, Duchamp's *Green Box* contains exact facsimiles of 93 documents, mostly old scraps of paper, recording his thoughts as he developed this climactic work. Signed copies of the *Box* are now valuable collectors' items. The *Glass*'s full title appears on the cover in French.

The Passage of the Virgin to the Bride, 1912

Study for *Virgin*, 1912

Three early works by Duchamp, all made during his Munich sojourn in 1912, provide an unusually clear guide to the development of his visual ideas for the *Large Glass*. Beginning with the *Virgin* (a study for which is at left), Duchamp introduced the notion of the human body as a mechanical sex object. In *The Passage of the Virgin to the Bride (above)*, he visualizes the "moment of change" from one state to another. And in *The Bride (above, right)*, a technically superb painting, he shows a fully realized, precisely mechanized being, thus completing the cycle.

Although both the actors and the action of *Passage* are difficult to determine, one critic, Lawrence D. Steefel, claims that he can see the Bride spreading across the canvas from lower left to upper right, her skirt, chest and even an arm "flung across an indistinct

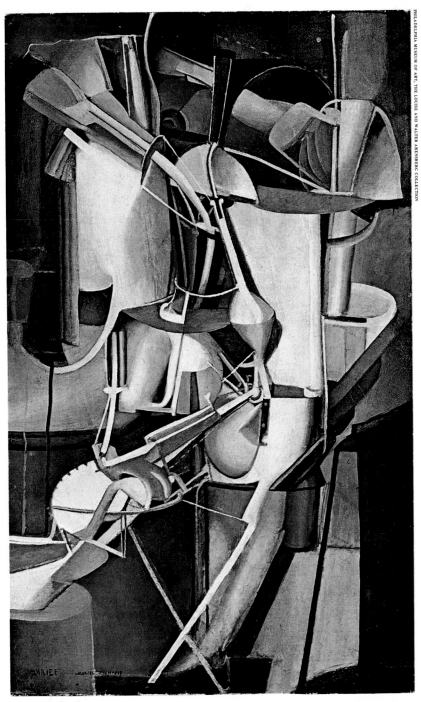

The Bride, 1912

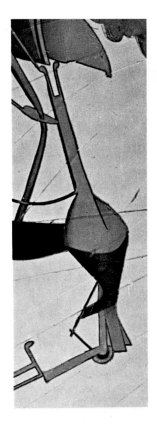

One clue to the imagery in these works is the form above, a significant detail from the Bride section of the *Large Glass* which Duchamp called the "wasp" or "sex cylinder." Notice its recurrence in *Passage* and *The Bride.* Below is a version of a male element, the realistically rendered *Chocolate Grinder*, which appears in the Bachelor half of the *Large Glass.*

face at the upper right corner." Duchamp, as usual, offered no corroboration and left it to the viewer to determine where the Bride is and what, if anything, is happening.

But more important than any real or imagined imagery are the ideas behind these works. Earlier, in *Portrait, Sad Young Man in a Train* and *Nude Descending a Staircase (pages 25-27)*, Duchamp had pictured, on a two-dimensional surface, figures in motion through time and space. Here, however, he was working with the far more abstract and intellectual concept of transmutation. More than just the physical act, Duchamp wanted to depict the once-in-a-lifetime, irreversible change from virginity to bridehood—a process which is almost, but not quite, consummated in *The Bride Stripped Bare by Her Bachelors, Even.*

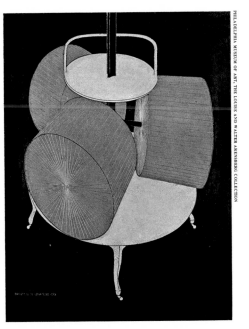

Chocolate Grinder, 1914

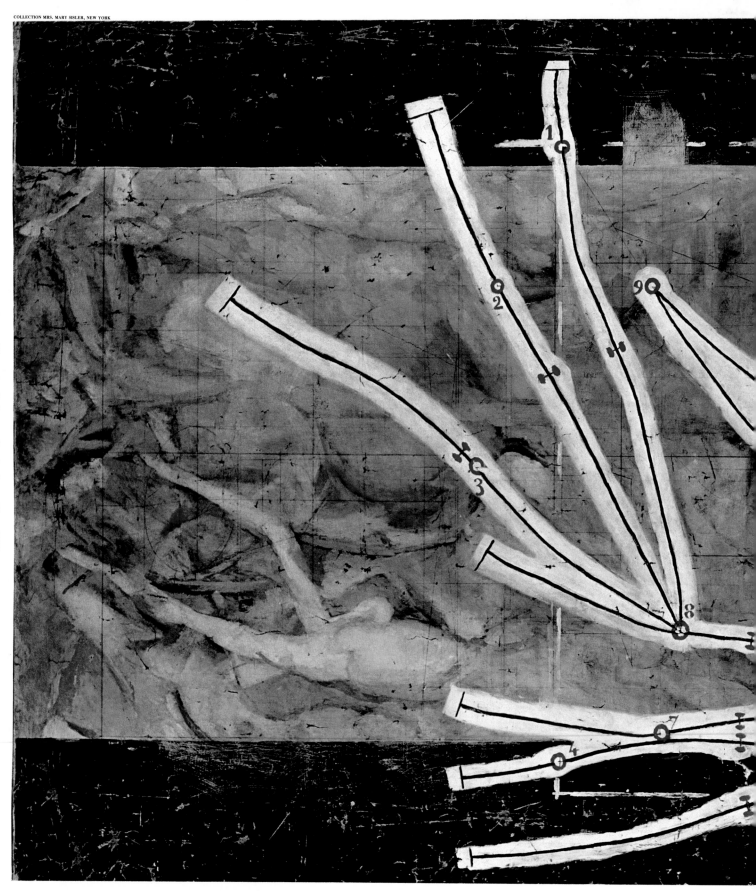

Viewpoint B: Layout for the *Large Glass*, 1913

Viewpoint C: *Network of Stoppages*, 1914

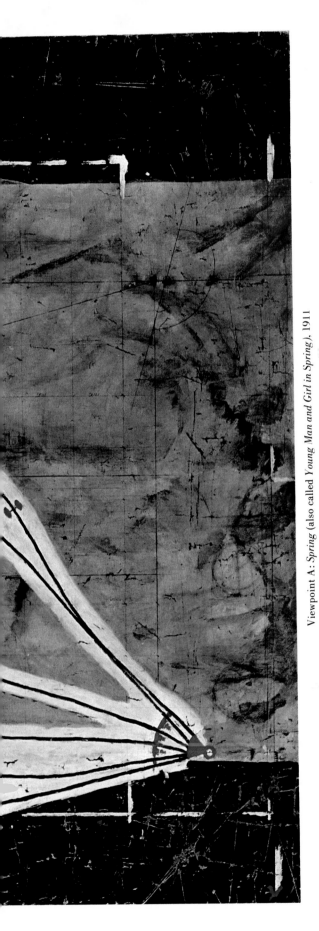

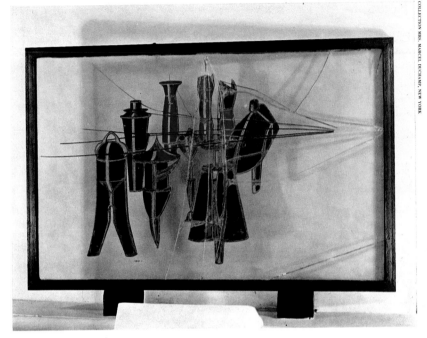

Nine Malic Molds, 1914-1915

The large, extraordinary painting at left is a composite of three works related to the *Large Glass*—a kind of topographical map. The elements may be singled out if the work is seen from three different points of view. From Viewpoint A, one can discern, near the top, the figures of a young girl and a man in joyous dance celebrating *Spring*, the title of the unfinished picture. This underlying work relates thematically —the sexual encounter between male and female—to the *Large Glass*. From Viewpoint B, a faint, pencil layout of the *Glass* can be seen, half actual size. The base canvas has been overpainted with two dark side panels to reduce its proportions to that of the *Glass*. The third element in the painting (seen from Viewpoint C) is the *Network of Stoppages*, which gives the whole work its title. These nine black lines —the "stoppage" is the standard unit of measurement in Duchampian physics—locate the exact positions for two important elements in the Bachelor section of the *Glass;* the capillary tubes and the malic molds. Duchamp devised these "rulers" by dropping three one-meter-long threads from a height of one meter and then tracing the random undulations to make three templates. These were traced three times to make the nine lines on the canvas. The numbered circles along the lines indicate positions for the malic molds. After this mapping on canvas, Duchamp made a preliminary version of the malic molds and capillary tubes, in his first work on glass *(above).* Duchamp kept it upon the mantle over the fireplace in his New York apartment.

Large Glass, 1915-1923 (photograph retouched for easier study)

A Guided Tour through the Strange World of "The Bride Stripped Bare by Her Bachelors, Even"

Using George Heard Hamilton's translation of Duchamp's notes on the *Large Glass* as the basis for his text, author Calvin Tomkins here takes the reader, step by step, through the various elements of Duchamp's masterpiece. His word of caution: "Though André Breton described this as 'a great modern legend,' Duchamp intended the *Large Glass* to be a 'hilarious' picture: those who approach it with too reverent an air will miss much, for it is rich in the comic spirit."

In examining the *Large Glass* it is best to begin with the Bachelors, and to work upward, observing one by one the elements of this curious machinery whose sole function is to make love. At the far left-hand side of the lower panel appear nine reddish-brown forms that at first glance resemble chessmen. These are

the malic molds, already familiar from the 1914 study on glass called *Neuf Moules Malic (Nine Malic Molds)*. They represent the Bachelors, but in a somewhat indirect manner: they are the outlines of hollow molds from which casts could be made, by pouring in lead or some other molten substance, of nine different male functionaries. Duchamp identifies these as priest, department store delivery boy, gendarme, cuirassier, policeman, undertaker's assistant, flunky, busboy and stationmaster. Each of these figures has an occupation for which there is no female equivalent—thus the Duchampian term "malic," which does not mean "masculine" (*mâle* in French) but rather "male-ish." The malic molds are drawn in vanishing-point perspective. Duchamp outlined them in lead wire and painted them with red lead, a "provisional color" applied "while waiting for each one to receive its color"—i.e., he preferred to leave the choice of a permanent color to chance and natural oxidation.

From the top of each mold, "capillary tubes" run toward the center of the *Glass*. These tubes follow the contours of the *Standard Stoppages*, and they all converge in the first of a series of seven funnels, or "sieves," which describe an arc in the middle of the panel. The last four sieves (which Duchamp also refers to at times as "parasols") are mottled and dark; their color comes from the dust that Duchamp allowed to breed on this part for six months, and then sealed in with varnish.

Directly beneath the sieves we find the "chocolate grinder," also recognizable from previous studies. The central location of this item and the references to it in Duchamp's notes leave little doubt as to its "malic" function. The grinder operates independently of the other elements of the Bachelor Machine, illustrating Duchamp's "adage of spontaneity," which states that "the bachelor grinds his chocolate himself." The chocolate, "coming from one knows not where," is ground between the rollers, where it leaves a deposit of "milk chocolate." Rising vertically from the top of this apparatus is a rod whose function seems to be fully as explicit as that of the grinder—it is called the "bayonet" and it supports a pair of large, X-shaped "scissors." But, as we will observe when we come to the operation of the Bachelor Machine, this sturdy bayonet does not perform at all in the manner we might expect, nor for that matter do any of the other elements. The dangers of a too-literal interpretation should be kept firmly in mind at all times.

Just to the left of the chocolate grinder and below the malic molds is the "glider," or "sleigh," a sort of carriage on runners, equipped with a "water wheel." The glider is driven by an "imaginary waterfall" (we do not see it) that supposedly falls on the water wheel; this turns the wheel and causes the glider to slide backward and forward on its runners with a jerky motion.

The remaining elements of the Bachelor apparatus are the "oculist witnesses," three circular designs that resemble the charts used to test one's vision, at the far right of the lower panel. Unlike the other elements which were outlined in lead wire or lead foil and then painted, the oculist witnesses were applied by an extremely delicate process of "silver scratching": Duchamp had the glass panel silvered on the back like a mirror, and he then scraped away everything but the intricate filaments of the

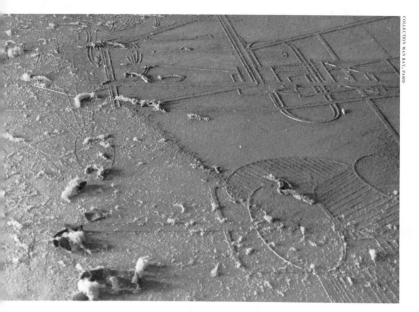

Dust Collecting, 1920

the capillary tubes at the top of each malic mold, which begin to converge toward the right.

As it passes through the tubes, the gas undergoes a physical change. Through "the phenomenon of stretching in the unit of length" (one of the laws of Duchamp's Playful Physics), it solidifies into long needles, which break up into "spangles of frosty gas" (also unseen) as soon as they emerge from the other end of the tube. The spangles tend to rise, being lighter than air, but they are caught as they emerge from the tubes by the first cone, or sieve. Duchamp does not hesitate to attribute to the spangles certain human characteristics. In their passage through the seven sieves, the last four of which are clogged with dust, they lose their "individuality." They undergo a further change of state caused by their temporary "dizziness," and at the end of their journey through the sieves they have become "a liquid elemental scattering." And, Duchamp concludes, in what could be either admiration or contempt, "What a drip!"

What happens next is a trifle unclear. In his notes, Duchamp makes reference to a complicated series of operations that transport the liquid drops by means of a "toboggan" to the area of the "splash," which is directly below the oculist witnesses. None of these operations appear visually in the *Glass,* simply because Duchamp never got around to depicting them. We can only assume that the drops, which have become by this time an ex-

design. He had used the same method in a small 1918 work with the arresting title *To Be Looked at with One Eye, Close to, for Almost an Hour,* a work that does not seem at first glance to be related to the *Large Glass,* until one realizes that it incorporates a small magnifying glass, placed there, Duchamp indicates, for the Peeping Tom who waits "while looking with one eye for almost an hour" for the disrobing of the Bride. This piece can now be found on the third floor of The Museum of Modern Art in New York, where Peeping Toms who squint into the magnifying glass may be somewhat disappointed to see, not the Bride stripped bare, but the image of Duchamp's *Fresh Widow,* which is on exhibit across the room.

The Bachelors, poor souls, are inferior in every way to the Bride. Some interpreters have seen the whole work as a satire on the deification of women in our society; while such interpretations may be far too logical, the Bachelors' servile and dependent status cannot be ignored. "The Bride has a life center," Duchamp tells us, "—the Bachelors have not. They live on coal or other raw material drawn not from them but from their not-them." The Bride commands, the Bachelors obey. Even their desire for her is activated by the Bride, who gives the signal for the malic molds to receive the "illuminating gas." This is the start of the Bachelors' lovemaking operations, which we will now attempt to follow, step by surprising step.

Upon receiving the illuminating gas, the malic molds "cast" it in their own respective forms (priest, gendarme, et cetera). No longer empty husks, these "gas castings" begin immediately to play their malic role, which is announced to them, appropriately enough, by a sort of masculine dirge. The melancholy sounds come from the glider, which, driven endlessly to and fro by the water falling on the wheel, emits this litany: "Slow life. Vicious circle. Onanism. Horizontal. Round trip for the buffer. Junk of life. Cheap construction. Tin, cords, iron wire. Eccentric wooden pulleys. Monotonous flywheel. Beer professor." The repetition of these dolorous words (descriptive perhaps of the bacheloric state) causes the illuminating gas to start flowing through

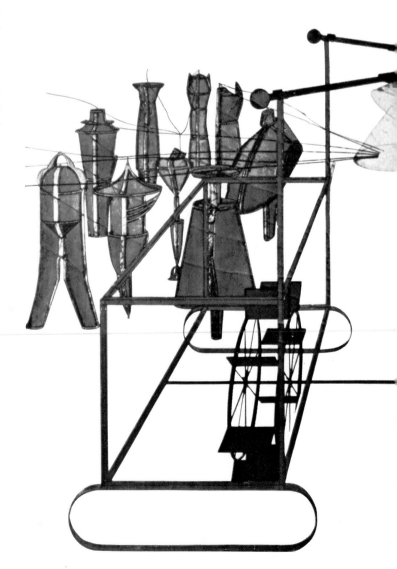

90

plosive liquid, somehow reach the splash area, where they are "dazzled" upward with terrific velocity through the center of the oculist witnesses and into the Bride's domain. With this "dazzling of the splash," the series of Bachelor operations ends.

Moving to the upper half of the *Large Glass (pages 92-93)*, we are struck first by the wholly different character of the forms there. In the Bachelor Machine, the principal forms are precise and geometrical—circles, rectangles, cones and the like. "In the Bride," Duchamp states, "the *principal forms* are *more or less large or small*, have no longer, in their relation to their destination, a mensurability . . . ." Here everything is imprecise and dreamlike. Anything has become possible, for the elements of desire are no longer merely mechanical and repetitive; they are the visual images of the Bride's imagination.

"The Bride is basically a motor," Duchamp informs us. But she is a far more complex motor than anything found in the Bachelors' quarters. In fact, she is an internal combustion engine. The ovoid shape at the lower left-hand side of the Bride panel is her "reservoir of love gasoline," a sort of "timid-power," or "auto-mobiline" which she herself secretes. The long, sticklike shape running from the reservoir almost to the division between the upper and lower panels is the Bride's "desire-magneto." Just above the reservoir is a "motor with quite feeble cylinders," which connects with the larger form at the top left that Duchamp

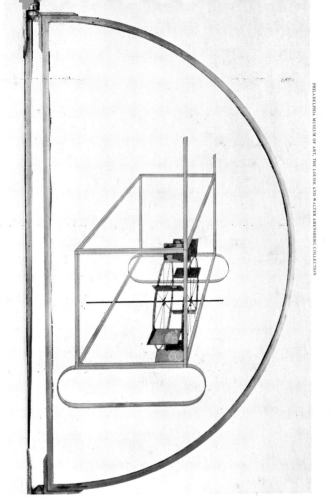

Glider Containing a Water Mill in Neighboring Metals, 1913-1915

has designated the "*pendu femelle*." The *pendu femelle* is to be considered the "skeleton" of the Bride herself and the seat of the ruling Bridal imagination.

Just to the right of the *pendu femelle*, we find a form that first appeared in Duchamp's 1912 painting *Bride*—a flask-shaped object, narrowing at the top and ending in a pair of horns. This is the "wasp," or "sex cylinder," the nerve center of the Bride's desire. And finally, floating across the top of the *Glass* like a large cloud is the "cinematic blossoming" of the Bride—not something emanating from the Bride but the Bride herself, represented "cinematically" at the moment of her own blossoming, which is also the moment of her being stripped bare. This cinematic blossoming, Duchamp informs us, is "the most important part of the painting," but once again we are warned not to look upon it with too literal an eye. "It is, in general, the halo of the Bride," he goes on to say, "the sum total of her splendid vibrations: graphically, there is no question of symbolizing by a grandiose painting this happy goal—the Bride's desire; only more clearly, in all this blossoming, the painting will be an inventory of the elements of this blossoming."

Two more visual elements must be mentioned. The cloud of the cinematic blossoming contains three windows, roughly square and of approximately equal size. These are the "draft pistons," which act as a kind of telegraph system to transmit the commands and instructions issued by the *pendu femelle*. To arrive at their particular shape, Duchamp utilized the force of wind—i.e., he hung a square of white gauze in an open window where it could be "accepted and rejected by the draft," photographed it three times, and reproduced the resulting wind-blown shapes

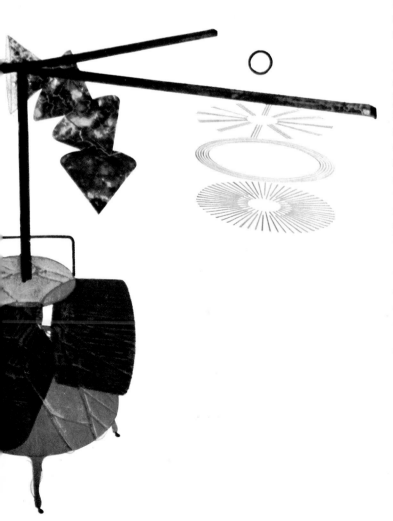

as his draft pistons. Just below the third piston and slightly to the right are nine small holes drilled in the *Glass*. These are the nine "shots," whose placement Duchamp arrived at by taking nine matches whose tips had been dipped in paint, and firing them at the *Glass* from three different points by means of a toy cannon. Duchamp thus invoked chance in still another way: having already used gravity *(Standard Stoppages)* and wind (draft pistons), he employed in this instance a factor that he termed "ordinary skill" to produce a pattern that had nothing to do with the artist's skill or taste. The function of the shots, as we shall see, is to bring the Bachelors' splash under Bridal control.

Before attempting to describe the intricate operations of the Bride-motor, we must go back a little to that moment of the splash. The droplets, we recollect, have been dazzled upward through the oculist witnesses into the Bride's realm. But these droplets do not reach the Bride directly. When they come into contact with the Bride's "clothing," which is represented by the three horizontal lines dividing the upper and lower parts of the *Glass*, they are deflected and thrown upward toward the nine shots. Here they become subject to the commands of the *pendu femelle*, transmitted by the draft pistons. In striking against the Bride's clothing, however, they activate a clockwork machine called the Boxing Match (another concept that Duchamp never got around to executing on the *Glass*), whose function is to help bring about, by electrical means, the fall of the Bride's clothes. The sparks of this "electrical undressing" ignite the love gasoline in the Bride's motor (the motor with quite feeble cylinders), and the blossoming begins.

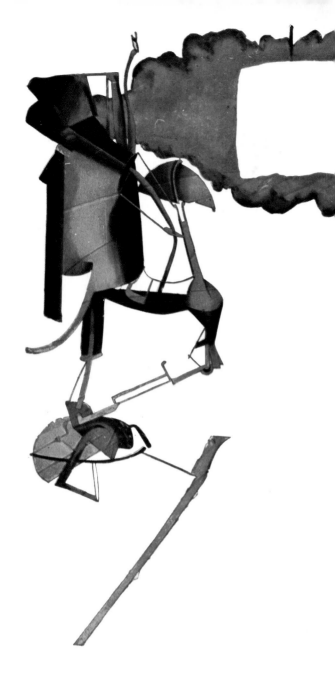

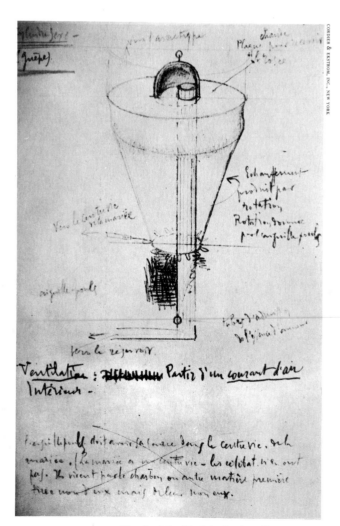

Sketch of the Sex Cylinder from the *Green Box*

The Bride, however, is no mere passive witness to her own stripping. Although Duchamp describes her as "an apotheosis of virginity," she has her quota of "ignorant desire," or "blank desire (with a touch of malice)," and because of this she "warmly rejects (not chastely) the Bachelors' brusque offer." Furthermore, she contributes voluntarily to the process by supplying sparks from her own desire-magneto to the motor with quite feeble cylinders. "The Bride accepts this stripping by the Bachelors, since she supplies the love gasoline to the sparks of this electrical stripping; moreover, she furthers her complete nudity by adding to the first focus of sparks (electrical stripping) the second focus of sparks of the desire-magneto." Thus a two-stroke internal combustion process is set in motion, the Bride both permitting and willing her own nudity, and "developing in a sparkling fashion" her own desire for fulfillment.

The notion of a mysterious female power that is both passive (permitting) and active (desiring) runs through all Duchamp's notes on the subject. The Bachelors, in fact, have virtually no say in the matter; they react subserviently to her desiring imagination. It is her "blank desire (with a touch of malice)" that transmits, through the draft pistons, the original order that

leaves a huge gap in the graphic realization of the artist's idea —it eliminates the "electrical stripping" and means, in effect, that the Bride is *not* stripped bare, after all.

As the *Large Glass* resists rational description, so it also resists critical interpretation. The first and perhaps the best analysis of it is still André Breton's 1935 essay *Phare de la Mariée* ("Lighthouse of the Bride"), in which he spoke of it poetically as "the trophy of a fabulous hunt through virgin territory, at the frontiers of eroticism, of philosophical speculation, of the spirit of sporting competition, of the most recent data of science, of lyricism, and of humor." The gallery owners Harriet and Sidney Janis have placed it within the traditional iconography of Christian art, writing in 1945 that the *Glass* "is essentially an Assumption of the Virgin composition, with the lower part given over to the secular world and its motivations, the upper, to the realm of the inner mechanism and inner spirit." Very few of our formal art critics have chosen to deal with the work at all, though, and Duchamp himself has provided no particular enlightenment. At one point he spoke of "having already passed a good part of my life in that fog behind the *Glass*," but more recently he was heard to say that "the *Glass* is not my autobiography, nor is it self-expression."

Certainly there has been nothing like it in the history of art, and there are no real standards by which it can be judged. Unfinished and infinitely complex, shattered and repaired, the *Glass* continues to work its spell on those who will submit to it, and casts its mysterious shadow far into the future.

starts the illuminating gas flowing into the malic molds in the Bachelor Machine. It is by her consent that the electrical stripping ignites the love gasoline in her engine. Stirred by the action of her "wasp," she supplies the sparks from her desire-magneto that set up the two-stroke internal combustion process in the motor with quite feeble cylinders, which in turn generates the power for her magical blossoming. And at the climactic moment of her blossoming she still reigns supreme, untouched and unconquered by the rude Bachelors, retaining her splendid power to accept their splash (which awaits its instructions from the draft pistons) or to reject it, as she pleases. The blossoming is the last state before fulfillment. But fulfillment—the act which might bring about her fall—never takes place. The Bride, like Keats's maiden on the Grecian urn, remains forever lovely and unravished, eternally in passage between desire and possession.

Such, in brief, is the drama of *The Bride Stripped Bare by Her Bachelors, Even.* The work defies rational description, of course, for no mere synopsis can begin to suggest the infinitely subtle ramifications of the notes or the intricate and phenomenal craftsmanship with which each visual detail is carried out. The omission of such an important element as the Boxing Match

Sketch of the Boxing Match from the *Green Box*

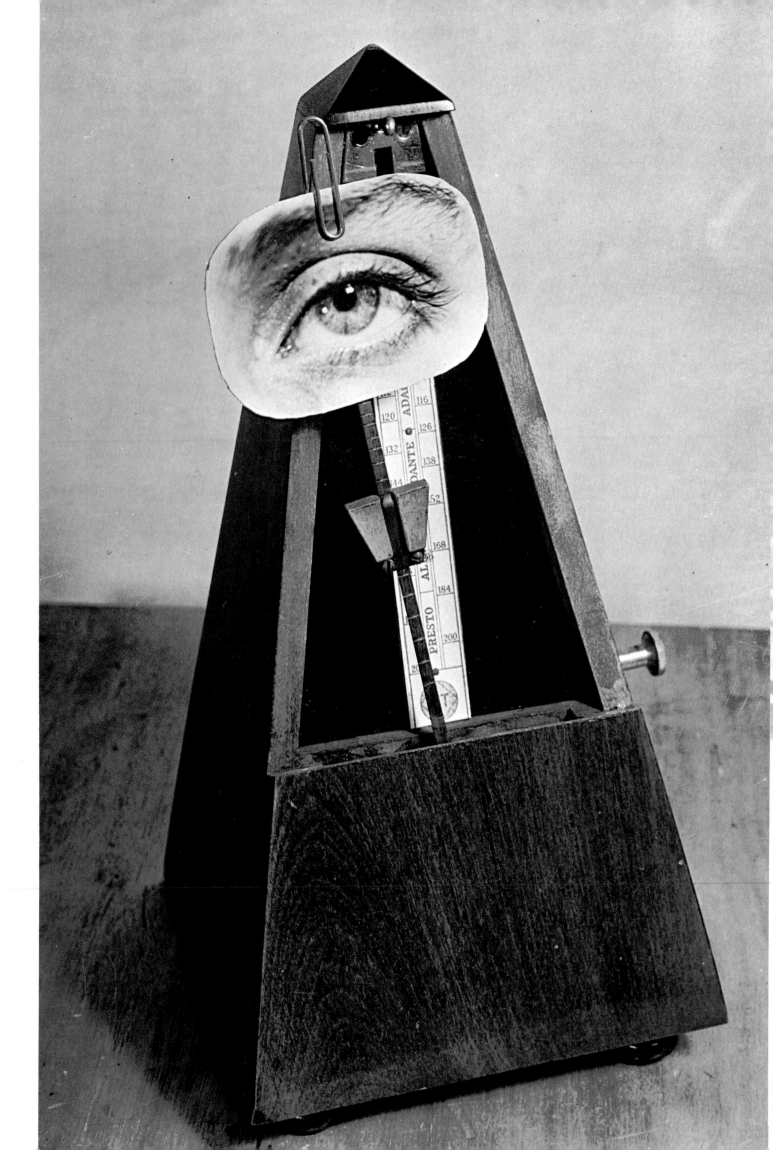

V

Surrealism's Dream World

At the time of this writing new shivers are running through the intellectual atmosphere; it requires only courage to face them.

—COMTE DE LAUTREAMONT, 1869

One evening in 1919, just as he was on the point of falling asleep, André Breton became aware of a strange phrase that had appeared at the edge of his conscious mind. The phrase—"There is a man cut in two by the window"—was accompanied by a faint visual apparition of a walking man cut off at waist level by a window. The image had a disturbing power, as images glimpsed in the state midway between dream and waking sometimes do, and Breton, a poet who would soon abandon his medical studies to devote full time to literature, immediately decided that it could be incorporated into his poetry. "I had no sooner invested it with that quality," he later wrote, "than it gave place to a succession of all but continuous sentences which left me no less astonished but in a state, I would say, of extreme detachment."

Breton was familiar with Freud's revolutionary methods of working with neurotic patients. It struck him that the Freudian "free association" and dream analysis techniques could perhaps be applied to other than psychoanalytic ends; that they might be used to provide rich new material for poetic construction. Together with his friend and fellow-poet Philippe Soupault, Breton began experimenting. They shut themselves up in a dark room, tried to simulate a semiconscious, dreamlike state of mind, and wrote down whatever words, images and sentences occurred to them. "By the end of the first day of the experiment we were able to read to one another about 50 pages obtained in this manner and to compare the results," Breton reported. "The likeness was on the whole striking. There were similar faults of construction, the same hesitant manner, and also, in both cases, an illusion of extraordinary verve, much emotion, a considerable assortment of images of a quality such as we would never have been able to obtain in the normal way of writing, a very special sense of the picturesque, and, here and there, a few pieces of outright buffoonery." Breton's summary is an excellent description of literary Surrealism, which grew out of the two young poets' experiments with automatic writing. These experiments were published in 1921, under the title *Les Champs Magnétiques (The Magnetic Fields)*, and thus became the first Surrealist text.

Man Ray's *Object to Be Destroyed* remained intact for almost 35 years —although Ray intended to destroy it—until a group of anti-Dada art students in Germany broke it while demonstrating at a Dada show. Shortly thereafter Ray reproduced the work and called it *Indestructible Object.*

Man Ray:
Object to Be Destroyed, 1923

It is difficult today to conceive of the excitement and the limitless hopes that attended the birth of Surrealism. The word itself has passed into common usage as an adjective to describe whatever seems wholly absurd or "wacky," and Breton's "outright buffoonery" would now be considered by many people an adequate description of the whole movement. Surrealism, however, was an intensely serious affair. Although it began as a literary method and achieved its greatest fame as a new school of painting, Surrealism always appeared to its founders as far more than that. It was to be a revolution in consciousness, whose avowed goal was "to change life" in the most profound manner possible, and its members committed themselves totally and passionately to this goal and to Breton, the movement's charismatic leader.

Revolutionary as it seemed at the time, Surrealism had clear historical antecedents. The most obvious of these was the Dada movement, in which nearly all the original Surrealists had played an active role. Breton's and Soupault's early experiments with automatic writing actually coincided with Dadaism's brief and riotous career in Paris. Both men were in the forefront of the Dada manifestations of 1920 and 1921, and it was Breton, as we have seen, who precipitated the disintegration of Dada in 1922 through his quarrel with Tristan Tzara over the proposed Congress of Paris. The ex-Dadaists who followed Breton into Surrealism retained from Dada their utter contempt for the logic and "good sense" of a society that had nearly destroyed itself in the First World War. For Dada's total nihilism, though, they substituted a profound faith in the unconscious nature of man. Inspired by the recent discoveries of Freud—whom Breton went to interview in Vienna in the summer of 1921—they looked upon the unconscious as a marvelous, undiscovered world of human experience, a world in which human reason did not play the commanding role and in which it was therefore possible to look for the means of total liberation for the human spirit. It was through man's unconscious mind, above all, that the Surrealists hoped to change life.

In literature, the Surrealists claimed descent from several different sources. They acknowledged a clear and immediate debt to the late Guillaume Apollinaire, whose incandescent, hallucinated poetry anticipated Surrealist verse, and who actually provided the movement with its name: Breton took the word from Apollinaire's 1917 play *Les Mamelles de Tirésias*, which was subtitled *drame surréaliste*. The Surrealists also discovered a common bond linking them in spirit with the Gothic novelists in 18th Century English literature—writers such as Horace Walpole and M. G. ("Monk") Lewis whose novels were steeped in an atmosphere of mysterious and irrational events, dreams, madness, cruelty and eroticism. The Surrealists' admiration for erotic adventuring also led them to make a hero of the infamous Marquis de Sade, whose career became for them a Gothic novel superior to anything in the genre. They found their direct progenitor, however, in Arthur Rimbaud, the French 19th Century poet who had scorned all literary and social conventions and in whose hands poetry ceased to be primarily a means of expression and became, instead, a method of discovery and

This unusual photograph of André Breton, taken by Man Ray in 1931, suggests some of the hypnotic qualities of his appearance at that time. Breton, the dictator of Surrealism, had a massive face, a swept-back mane, and a chilling gaze. His masklike countenance rarely relaxed in a smile. "It is Breton's violence," wrote Adrienne Monnier, "that makes him statuesque. He brings to mind a medieval sword-bearer and has the rapt immobility of a medium."

divination. "I say that one must be a *seer*, one must make oneself a seer," Rimbaud had written in 1871, and he went on to describe how it was done: "The poet becomes a seer by a long, enormous and reasoned *derangement of all his senses.* . . . He seeks himself, he exhausts in himself every poison, retaining only their quintessences. Ineffable torture, in which he requires supreme faith, superhuman strength, in which he becomes among all men the great invalid, the great criminal, the great accursed—and the supreme sage!"

Rimbaud had charted the course that the Surrealists were determined to follow, but the real model for Surrealist literature was provided by another writer, a man whose strange career is appropriately buried in mystery. Only the barest facts are known about Isidore Ducasse, who chose to call himself the Comte de Lautréamont. He was born in 1846 in Montevideo, Uruguay, where his father held a French consular post. He came to France to finish his schooling at a lycée in the Basses-Pyrénées, and in 1865 he made his way to Paris, where he died of unknown causes in 1870, at the age of 24. During the five years he lived in Paris, supposedly preparing himself to enter the Ecole Polytechnique, Lautréamont composed a long and altogether extraordinary work, in a prose that comes close to poetry, called *Les Chants de Maldoror.* Grotesque, turgid, startlingly beautiful and highly blasphemous, the book contains some of the most remarkable flights of imagination ever put on paper—in one scene, which takes place during a tempest at sea, the superhuman Maldoror slakes his craving for absolute evil by murdering the sole survivor of a shipwreck, then plunges into the maelstrom and has sexual intercourse with a gigantic female shark. It is strewn throughout with images that are supremely Surrealist, such as the memorable "handsome as the retractability of the claws of birds of prey" and the astonishing description of a young man, "beautiful as the chance meeting upon a dissecting table of a sewing machine and an umbrella!" Breton discovered the work quite by accident and immediately made it required reading for every member of the Surrealist group.

Whether or not these antecedents would have produced the Surrealist movement without the guiding personality of André Breton is doubtful. For more than 40 years he has exercised his iron will over every phase of the movement, and at times the dissenting factions have been held together only by the force of his personality. Descriptions of him in the early days of the movement all stress his extraordinary personal magnetism. "He was good-looking, with a beauty not angelic but archangelic," according to the bookseller Adrienne Monnier. Breton infuriated many people with his haughty, humorless and uncompromising manner, and his friends never knew when they might fall from favor, but while it lasted his friendship was a rare gift. According to Maurice Nadeau, the historian of the movement, "Those who enjoyed the moments of his unforgettable friendship, which he begrudged no one, were ready to sacrifice everything to him: wife, mistresses, friends; and some, in fact, did sacrifice these things. They gave themselves entirely to him and to the movement."

While Dadaism performed its own last rites in Paris, the young French

GUILLAUME APOLLINAIRE

Born in Rome and educated in France, Guillaume Apollinaire, shown here in a cubist portrait by his friend Louis Marcoussis, became a leader of the avant-garde poets and painters of Paris in the years before World War I. He believed that poets should develop an eye for the exciting resemblances of disparate things. Before his death in 1918, Apollinaire published two important collections of his poems, *Alcools* (1913) and *Calligrammes* (1918).

poets and writers who had grouped themselves around Breton plunged enthusiastically into all kinds of Surrealist experiments. They practiced automatic writing, transcribed their dreams and took part in spiritualistic sessions at which the individual members would speak, write or draw while under hypnosis. This so-called "period of trances" was inaugurated by the poet René Crevel, who had learned the technique from a professional medium. Robert Desnos, the acknowledged star of their sessions, could fall into a trance and "speak his dreams" with a virtuosity that struck some outsiders as slightly suspect; his most surprising accomplishments in this vein were the extremely complex puns, anagrams and other bits of wordplay that he produced when, under hypnosis, he claimed to have entered the mind and imagination of Duchamp's imaginary alter-ego, Rrose Sélavy. The experiments took place in an atmosphere of mounting excitement. As the writer Louis Aragon described the period, "It was a time when, meeting in the evening like hunters after a day in the field, we made the day's accounting, the list of beasts we had invented, of fantastic plants, of images bagged."

By the fall of 1924, Breton felt that matters were far enough advanced to launch the new movement formally. In his "First Surrealist Manifesto" which appeared that year, Breton defined Surrealism as "pure psychic automatism, by which it is intended to express, verbally, in writing, or by other means, the true function of thought—thought dictated in the absence of all control exercised by reason and outside all esthetic or moral preoccupations." The movement's goal and purpose he described as "the future resolution of those two seemingly contradictory states, dream and reality, in a kind of absolute reality, surreality, so to speak."

The early development of Surrealism was so dominated by literary men that one might well ask what all this experimentation had to do with the art of painting. It was a question that the Surrealists often debated among themselves. In his first manifesto, Breton had made only passing mention, in a footnote, of artists whose work might be said to contain evidence of psychic automatism, and as late as 1925 the Surrealists were still arguing whether painting could ever be Surrealist. In that year, however, Breton began a series of essays on modern artists that were to appear over the next two years in *La Révolution Surréaliste*, the movement's official journal, under the title "Surrealism and Painting." Among the artists who fulfilled Breton's requirements of "pure psychic automatism" were several such as Ernst, Arp, André Masson, and Yves Tanguy, who were already following a more or less Surrealist approach to painting, and others, notably Picasso, who would never officially join the movement. Breton also detected Surrealist antecedents in the fantastic art of previous periods—the *Caprichos* of Goya, for example, or the 16th Century double-image landscapes and portraits that were revealed on examination to be made up of painted fruits and vegetables. And in the contemporary Italian painter Giorgio de Chirico, born in 1880, Breton discovered an artist who was to Surrealist painting what Lautréamont had been to Surrealist poetry.

"There are many more enigmas in the shadow of a man who walks in the sun than in all the religions of the past, present, and future." For Giorgio de Chirico whose statement this is, painting was primarily a means of evoking the mysteries that lay at the heart of existence. Even the titles of his paintings echo this theme: *The Enigma of an Autumn Afternoon, The Enigma of the Hour, The Enigma of a Day*—pictures in which the menacing, arcaded streets of an Italian town are always deserted, the time is always late afternoon, and there is always the sense of some unimaginable event about to take place.

Many of de Chirico's graphic images can be traced to their unconscious source. The mysterious locomotives that appear in so many of his early works relate back to his lonely childhood in the Greek coastal province of Thessaly, where his father, an engineer, had been engaged in building a railroad line. The looming arcades of the architectural paintings have been interpreted as obsessive symbols of his mother, who exercised total domination over the sickly, melancholy Giorgio and his younger brother Andrea, a musician who later took the name Alberto Savinio. Thanks to Signora de Chirico's ambitions for her sons, Giorgio received a thorough academic training in art, first in Athens and later in Munich, where they moved soon after the father's death in 1905. The young man, however, gave no evidence of unusual talent until they moved again, to Florence, in 1910. It was here that he started to paint the "enigmas," characterized by meticulous realism of detail coupled with strange distortions of perspective that gave his pictures their prophetic, emotionally charged atmosphere. When de Chirico exhibited several of these works at both the 1913 Salon des Indépendants and the Salon d'Automne in Paris, they were immediately hailed by Apollinaire, who proclaimed him "the most astonishing painter of the younger generation." Apollinaire befriended de Chirico, who had moved to Paris, and probably suggested to him a number of his evocative titles.

After a period of inactivity due to illness, de Chirico began to paint new works whose subject matter was still largely architectural, but in which locomotives often appeared or were suggested by their smoke. These were followed by his "tower series," which culminated in the magnificent *Nostalgia of the Infinite (page 115)*, one of his most beautiful paintings, whose central structure was probably suggested by the soaring Mole Antonelliana in Turin where he had stayed for a short time in 1911. Next came a series of paintings in which classical statuary was juxtaposed with strangely out-of-scale everyday objects—huge artichokes, giant fruits. He also continued to paint in the vein of his earlier cityscapes, producing such masterpieces as *The Mystery and Melancholy of a Street* and *The Enigma of a Day*, two paintings which made a strong impression on the Surrealists. *The Enigma of a Day* hung for several years in Breton's studio on the Rue Fontaine, where the Surrealists used it as a stimulant to their subconscious researches; they referred to it as "an inhabitable dream." After 1914, though, architecture figured less prominently in his work. He embarked on a series of still lifes in which inanimate objects seemed to take on an ominous, spectral character, and he began also to paint the famous mannequins—armless tailor's dummies whose smooth, featureless faces sometimes bore, in

A poet with a strong visual sense, Apollinaire designed this poem, *"Il Pleut"* ("It's Raining"), to present a picture of its subject. He made other poems in the shapes of flowers, trees and insects. These experiments with pictorial typography were meant to show what happens to language when it is presented visually and what becomes of an abstract image when it is endowed with literary meaning.

place of eyes, the symbols for infinity. The mannequin paintings reached their climax with *The Disquieting Muses (page 115)*, in 1917, probably his best-known work and, according to the American scholar James Thrall Soby, possibly "the greatest painting of de Chirico's entire career."

By this time, though, the War had intervened. De Chirico returned to Italy in 1915. Mobilized into the army, then sent to a convalescent hospital near Ferrara when his health broke down, he spent his time painting a new series known today as "the metaphysical interiors"—rooms filled with engineers' drawing instruments, maps, and sometimes, unaccountably, with enlarged replicas of the rolls and biscuits that he often saw in the windows of Jewish bakery shops in Ferrara. Carlo Carrà, an artist who had belonged to the Italian Futurist group before the War, was also a patient in the Ferrara hospital at this time. He became friendly with de Chirico, whose style had an influence on his own, and together they founded what they called the *scuola metafisica*, or metaphysical school of painting. They soon quarrelled and went their separate ways, but their work and ideas attracted considerable attention for a while and several of their metaphysical paintings were reproduced in the newly founded Italian art journal *Valori Plastici*, where they were seen and studied by future Surrealists like Max Ernst, in Cologne, and René Magritte, in Brussels.

De Chirico had his first postwar show of paintings in Rome in 1919. It was a dismal failure. Only one painting was sold, a nonmetaphysical portrait. Soon after this, his painting began to undergo a fundamental change. He "discovered" the art of the Italian Renaissance, and spent weeks copying the old masters in the museums. An academic quality appeared in his pictures, which were characterized now by muddy colors and unconvincing technical flourishes, and whose subjects were often taken from myths and legends such as *The Departure of the Argonauts* or *Hector and Andromache*. Ironically, just at the time that his early work was being hailed with such enthusiasm by Breton and the Surrealists, de Chirico's painting was in the process of losing those qualities of hallucinated imagery and unconscious enigma that had made him a proto-Surrealist.

De Chirico returned to Paris in 1925. He was welcomed by the Surrealists, who nevertheless let him understand their distaste for his current productions and urged him to return to his prewar style. His angry refusal to do so led to increasingly embittered relations. In 1926, Breton published a vitriolic attack on him in *La Révolution Surréaliste*, accompanied by a reproduction of de Chirico's recent canvas *Orestes and Electra* on which the editors had all scribbled with black pencil to show what they thought of it. This was the signal for even more savage attacks by Aragon and other Surrealists, to which de Chirico replied with fury. He denounced as worthless the entire field of modern art, including his own previous work; in fact, he even dismissed some of his pre-1922 paintings as forgeries!

The denouncement is one of the unsolved enigmas of modern art. De Chirico returned to Italy, where he has continued until the present day to paint uninspired, academic pictures that are not even very proficient technically, and where, it is said, he occasionally turns out, purely for funds, a "forgery" of his early manner. Although the Surrealists found much to admire in de Chirico's poetic, autobiographical novel *Hebdomeros*, published in 1929, they had only contempt for his post-1922 work. These paintings, says Soby, "are tiresomely sweet, even chic, and with them it seems fair to take leave of de Chirico as a vital force in modern art."

At about the time de Chirico's work was entering the first stages of its decline, in 1920, Max Ernst happened to see a de Chirico painting called *The Sacred Fish* in a Cologne exhibition. Although the picture was not one of de Chirico's best, it made a powerful impression on Ernst and helped to reinforce his progress in the direction that would soon bring him into the forefront of the Surrealist movement.

Max Ernst was born in 1891 in the town of Brühl, near Cologne. Although from childhood on he showed remarkable talent for drawing and painting, he never attended an art school, choosing instead to study philosophy at the University of Bonn. He survived four years in an artillery unit during the First World War, during which he was wounded twice in the head—once by the recoil of a gun and the other time from a mule's kick—and several times was almost court-martialed for insubordination. Ernst became an active Dadaist after the War, as we have seen. He also resumed painting, and in his pictures dating from 1920 or 1921, notably the collage-drawing *The Hat Makes the Man* and the nightmarish *Elephant of the Celebes (page 116)*, "Dadamax" appeared to be moving from Dada nihilism toward a more constructive use of unconscious material.

What first brought Ernst to the Surrealists' attention, though, were the collages that he began to make "one rainy day in 1919," when he became fascinated by the illustrations in an old scientific catalogue that he was idly leafing through. Under the scrutiny of his active imagination, the medical, paleontological and anthropological drawings and engravings provoked "a sudden intensification of the visionary faculties in me and brought forth an illusive succession of contradictory images, double, triple and multiple images, piling up on each other with the persistence and rapidity which are peculiar to love-memories and visions of half-sleep." The sensation—so strikingly similar to Breton's first experience with automatic phenomena—led Ernst to a whole series of experiments with illustrations clipped from scientific journals, children's books, Victorian magazines and other sources, which he then altered slightly by drawing over them, or combined with other cut-out images glued down in proximity to them, in such a way as to evoke the most fantastic dislocations of visual meaning. Collage, which Picasso and Braque had invented in 1912 and used for purely plastic purposes, became for Ernst a means of unconscious exploration and discovery, a method, as he put it, of "forcing inspiration."

To Ernst, collage was "an alchemic product" which depended for its primary effect upon disorientation or *displacement*. With his uncanny skill at manipulating images so as to produce a distinct mental jolt from their juxtaposition, he created such disturbing collages as *The Prepara-*

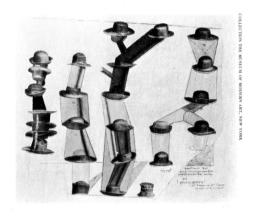

The curious collage-drawings of Max Ernst gave Surrealism a much-needed infusion of vigor in 1920. The one above, among his first, is titled *The Hat Makes the Man*, and was inspired by a hallucination Ernst had in a restaurant in Cologne: he claimed he saw the hats and coats hanging on a rack get up and move to another rack.

tion of Glue from Bones and *The Little Tear Gland That Says Tic Tac,* pictures whose titles increased the viewer's sense of disorientation.

Ernst had a one-man show of his collages in Paris in 1920. In the winter of 1922, with neither papers nor money, he came to Paris and was received with great enthusiasm by the Surrealists. The poet Paul Eluard and his Russian-born wife, Gala, were so warmly enthusiastic, in fact, that Ernst, who had left his own wife and son in Cologne, soon moved in to form a *ménage à trois*—a situation that Eluard accepted with studied unconcern, saying, "I love Max Ernst much more than I do Gala." The Surrealists refused on principle to respect bourgeois conventions regarding love and marriage, just as they refused to accept any limitations of human freedom. Besides which, no one could blame Gala for falling in love with Max. "Ernst was slender and carried himself very straight," Matthew Josephson wrote of him in that period: "He had a thin Roman nose, keen blue eyes, and an alert, birdlike air. Although just turned thirty-one his curly, gold-brown hair was slightly flecked with gray; he was altogether of an extraordinary male beauty —that of a 'fallen angel,' the women used to say."

One of the favorite Surrealist games during this "intuitive" period of the movement was the creation of "exquisite corpses," which could be either verbal or visual. The verbal form was a sentence composed by three or more persons, each of whom was assigned a specific part to write (subject, verb, predicate, etcetera) but none of whom knew what the others had written. The game took its name from the first such sentence composed in this manner, which read, "The exquisite/corpse/ shall drink/the bubbling wine." In a visual "exquisite corpse," each person drew something on a sheet of paper and then folded the sheet so the next person could not see what form the drawing had taken. Ernst collaborated energetically in these and other manifestations of Surrealist research, while continuing to look on "as a spectator" at the birth of his collages, drawings and paintings. His work of this period reached a high point with the well-known *Two Children Are Threatened by a Nightingale (page 117),* an oil painting on a wooden panel, with wooden collage elements.

In the summer of 1925, Ernst discovered a new means of forcing inspiration. Placing a sheet of paper on the rough floor boards of a seaside inn where he was staying, he rubbed the back of the paper with a soft pencil and found, by gazing attentively at the resulting drawings, that he was able to perceive a "hallucinatory succession of contradictory images." He experimented with rubbings of other materials— leaves, thread, the ragged edges of a piece of linen—and found that the drawings made in this way lost the character of the material employed and assumed a wholly new aspect. They became human heads, animals, gods, monsters, "a battle that ended with a kiss." The first fruits of this new method, which Ernst called *frottage* (rubbing) appeared in 1926 in an album of drawings entitled *Natural History.* Ernst maintained that *frottage* made it possible for him to exclude from his drawings all conscious intention and taste, and that it was therefore the exact equivalent of automatic writing. Of course, it was what Ernst

Four artists made this drawing in the Surrealist game called "The Exquisite Corpse." Yves Tanguy began this sketch at the top. He then folded the paper and handed it to Joan Miró, who could see only the lines where Tanguy had ended. Max Morise and Man Ray completed the drawing. André Breton explained: "What thrilled us in these productions was the certainty that, for better or worse, they stood for something that couldn't possibly be the work of a single brain, and possess to an exceptional degree that quality of drift which means so much to poetry."

did with the images obtained by rubbing that gave to each picture its true effect. The principle involved was not new; in fact, it came rather close to the one described by Leonardo da Vinci in his *Treatise on Painting*, where he recommended to his fellow artists that they could quicken "the spirit of invention" by staring fixedly at the stains and discoloration on old walls, until they discovered there "divine landscapes . . . battles and strange figures in violent action, expression of faces, and clothes, and an infinity of things." Ernst's *frottages* have nevertheless been generally accepted as the real beginning of Surrealism in the graphic arts. He soon found that the same method could be adapted to oil painting, and many of his unique and disquieting pictures of the 1920s, such as *Young People Trampling Their Mother*, *The Horde* and *Vision Provoked by the Nocturnal Aspects of the Porte St. Denis*, are the results of imagery obtained by *frottage*. Such methods, Ernst wrote, had "enabled painting to travel . . . a long way from Renoir's three apples, Manet's four sticks of asparagus, Derain's little chocolate women, and the Cubists' tobacco packet, and to open up for it a field of *vision* limited only by the *irritability capacity of the mind's powers.*"

Ernst's growing reputation soon got him into trouble with Breton. In 1926 Ernst accepted a commission from Sergei Diaghilev to design the stage sets for the ballet *Romeo and Juliet*, in collaboration with the Spanish painter Joan Miró. Breton was infuriated. The Surrealists were not supposed to let their researches be contaminated by contact with people like Diaghilev, whose Ballets Russes represented the most fashionable bourgeois modernism. Breton and Aragon published a pamphlet condemning the two artists for un-Surrealistic activities, and on the ballet's opening night the Surrealists staged a public protest. As the curtain went up on the Ernst-Miró set (and before the dancers appeared), the Surrealists in the audience began yelling insults and blowing whistles and noisemakers, and they kept at it until they were thrown out by the police. Ernst refused to take offense, and remained on terms of friendship with Breton. From then on, though, he pursued his own course, allied with the movement but not bound by the party line.

Surrealism had already become a powerful magnet by the time of Breton's "First Surrealist Manifesto" in 1924, attracting artists of extremely diverse temperaments. The career of Joan Miró, which we will follow in some detail in the next chapter, reached its critical turning point at that time when Miró made contact with the Paris Surrealists. André Masson had gone through a similar conversion slightly earlier. Badly wounded in the War, Masson painted for the next five years in a severe, somber style directly influenced by the Cubism of Juan Gris. His discovery of Surrealism released a flood of unconscious energy. Masson actually found that he could make automatic drawings, in much the same way that Breton and the poets practiced automatic writing, simply by letting his pen move across the paper according to its own "inner rhythm." He once made 22 drawings in a single day on the primary Surrealist theme of Desire. In his paintings, Masson would sometimes squeeze glue out on the canvas and spread sand over it to make abstract background shapes, on which he then painted recognizable

André Masson's passionate temperament and free-flowing drawing style are evident in *Animals Devouring Themselves*, a pastel which he made in 1928. Most of Masson's work deals with the violent side of nature, especially man's destructive instinct, but he has also illustrated the ancient myths of birth and desire in canvases that H. G. Wells once called "dream machines."

but distorted and disturbing images—fighting fish, rapacious birds, severed hands. A sense of physical violence marks all Masson's work; some of his later canvases, which he used to lay flat on the floor so as to be able to "paint with movement of the whole body," clearly anticipated the so-called "action painting" that Jackson Pollock and others evolved in the 1940s.

Jean Arp and Yves Tanguy, on the other hand, made relatively little use of automatism. Arp, a member of the original Zurich Dada group, had stayed on in Switzerland for several years after the War, arriving in Paris with his wife Sophie Taeuber in 1926. In his continuing search for the "symbols of metamorphosis and the future of human bodies," he had concentrated his attention on four basic forms—the egg (representing the world), the seed (identity), the cloud (water "on the loose") and the navel (a focal point and also, for Arp, a lunar symbol)—which he carved in wood and glued in various combinations to wooden backgrounds to form his "reliefs." Arp's belief in chance, "the highest and deepest of laws," gave his work a basis in common with Surrealism, but the fact was that his *use* of chance took him in another direction, toward a simple, natural world of forms in which nothing could ever be disoriented. When he realized this, about 1928, he quietly withdrew from active participation in the movement.

For Yves Tanguy, Surrealism and painting were inseparable. Born in 1900, Tanguy had made his living as a merchant seaman for two years when he happened to see one day, in the window of a Paris art gallery, a painting by de Chirico. Almost immediately, he said, he decided to become a painter. He never received any formal instruction. Befriended by Maurice Duhamel, a Surrealist film actor and translator of American literature, Tanguy moved into a dingy apartment behind the Gare Montparnasse, at 54 Rue du Château, and began to paint his luminous interior landscapes. The influence of de Chirico was clearly evident in Tanguy's use of forced perspective to create emotion, and in his effects of light and shadow. He experimented with automatism, making "exquisite corpses" with the others and sometimes turning his canvases upside down and working on them that way, to get a fresh perspective outside his own conscious intention. But Tanguy did not really need automatism in order to reach his unconscious. The milky white light of his pictures, the biomorphic shapes that often suggest the prehistoric menhirs and dolmens of his native Brittany, and the peculiar urgency of titles such as *Mama, Papa Is Wounded! (page 119)* are the work of one who found his own interior landscapes more convincing—and perhaps more real—than the world of fact and reason.

With the appearance of the Belgian René Magritte, who came to Paris in 1927 and immediately joined the Surrealist group, a new possibility revealed itself. Magritte proved that precise realism could be as Surrealist as pure automatism.

Born in 1898 in the town of Lessines, Magritte received a conventional grounding at the Academy of Fine Arts in Brussels. After a brief flirtation with abstract art, he fell under the influence of de Chirico and "found" as he said, "his first real painting in 1924. It represented a window seen from inside a room. On the other side of the window, a hand seems to be trying to grasp a flying bird." Everything Magritte did since that time was a deliberate act of visual disorientation. Taking utterly familiar, even banal objects and scenes as his subject matter, he painted them with painstaking attention to naturalistic detail and then placed them in situations where their very familiarity intensified the resulting mental jolt. In one of his paintings, the rear wall of a fireplace is pierced by a locomotive emerging at full speed. In others, nude women have fish heads (like mermaids in reverse), men in bowler hats descend like rain upon a quiet street, giant rocks float in mid-air. "I make a point (as far as possible) of painting only pictures that evoke the mystery of all existence with the precision and charm essential to the life of thought," Magritte has written. "It seems clear that precise and charming evocations of that mystery are furnished best by images of everyday objects combined or transformed in such a way that their agreement with our preconceived ideas, simple or sophisticated, is obliterated." As one critic observed, it was as though Magritte was "determined to fight reason with her own weapons."

Though Marc Chagall was never "officially" included in the Surrealist movement, the poetic fantasy and dreamlike quality of his images, in which "the Marvelous is always beautiful," conform to André Breton's dictum for Surrealism. This self-portrait is one of 20 sketches Chagall made to illustrate his autobiography.

All these diverse tendencies were presented to the public in the group exhibitions of Surrealism held from 1925 on in Paris, where they were shown together with the work of other artists who had never joined the movement but who seemed to share some of its preoccupations. It was a fact of some embarrassment to Breton that the best Surrealist painting so often seemed to be done by artists who were only peripherally Surrealist. The Swiss-born Paul Klee, whose graphic symbolism sprang from dreams, from children's drawings and from his own "prime realm of psychic improvisation," was included in the first collective Surrealist exhibition in 1925, and his work was frequently reproduced in *La Révolution Surréaliste.* Discussing Klee's painting in 1930, René Crevel wrote that "here, indeed, is the most intimate and precise surreality." But Klee took no part in organized Surrealism. In fact his drive to intellectualize his own largely instinctual art led him in 1921 to become a teacher at the Bauhaus in Weimar (later in Dessau), an establishment, as the critic Marcel Jean points out, that "could hardly be considered a Temple of the Unconscious." The Surrealists were also enthusiastic about the fanciful and poetic art of Marc Chagall, who had been painting in Paris before the War and had then returned to his native Russia, where he was caught by the Revolution. Appointed Minister of Art in Vitebsk, his native town, by the Communist government, he soon became disillusioned and left the country, returning in 1923 to Paris. The Surrealists had discovered his work by then, and they hailed him as a kindred spirit. With Chagall, Breton wrote, "the metaphor made its triumphant return into modern painting." Chagall's joyously emotional evocations of Russian village life made a deep impression on Max Ernst, among others, but Chagall himself chose to remain aloof from the movement. "I want an art of the earth," he said once, "and not merely an art of the head."

The one painter above all others whom the Surrealists wanted to annex was Picasso. Breton spoke of him in *Surrealism and Painting* as "the man from whom we persist in expecting more than from anyone else," and in the same essay he went so far as to suggest that the whole future of Surrealism depended on him: "It is now 15 years since Picasso began to explore this path, bearing rays of light with him as he went. . . . A single failure of will power on his part would be sufficient for everything we are concerned with to be at least put back, if not wholly lost." The frank hero-worship of Surrealism's leader had no appreciable effect on Picasso. It is true that there were Surrealist overtones in some of his paintings of the 1930s, but Surrealism never displaced his grapplings with wholly different styles, and he never assumed the role that Breton so hopefully offered him—that of guide and resident genius.

Duchamp's interest in chance—previously expressed in his *Three Standard Stoppages* and in parts of the *Large Glass*—led him to devise a system for playing roulette. To try it out, he capitalized himself and designed an issue of 30 bonds which he offered at 500 francs each. The bond certificate features a Man Ray photograph of Duchamp, bearded and horned with shaving lather. Although he sold only two bonds, Duchamp was able to spend a month in Monte Carlo. He broke even, a result which satisfied him perfectly. The bonds are now collector's items.

And what of Marcel Duchamp? He had returned quietly to Paris in 1923, after leaving his *Large Glass* in its state of "definitive incompletion." The following year he appeared, nude save for a fig leaf, in the single performance of Picabia and Satie's ballet *Relâche* that was in effect the last gasp of Dadaism (Duchamp also appeared with Man Ray, Picabia and Satie in the short, hilarious film *Entr'acte* by Picabia and René Clair, which was shown during the intermission of *Relâche*). He spent some time perfecting a system of playing roulette in which "one neither wins nor loses," and formed a one-man company to exploit the system at Monte Carlo. His "capital" came from the sale of stock certificates designed by Duchamp and bearing his image, in a photo by Man Ray that showed him with his long hair soaped into a pair of horns—the certificates, signed by Rrose Sélavy as Chairman of the Board, are now extremely valuable. In 1925 he completed a second optical machine, the *Rotary Demi-sphere*, which rotated a convex drawing of black and white spirals, placed on slightly different axes so that one spiral seemed to come forward while the other went back, and the following year he collaborated with Man Ray on the film *Anemic Cinema*, which alternated shots of similar spirals in action and titles composed of Duchamp's elaborate puns and anagrams.

When both his parents died, within a single week in 1925, Duchamp used his modest inheritance to make a few speculative purchases in the art market—an activity then engaged in by many of the Surrealists. In 1926 he visited New York to arrange an American show for the sculptor Brancusi whose work he admired, at the Brummer Gallery. Later, with his friend H. P. Roché he bought at auction a large collection of Brancusi's sculptures. From then on, whenever he needed funds, he sold one of the Brancusis. Duchamp's aim in life at this point was simply to break even. Only by having little money and few wants, he felt, was one free to do as he pleased.

More and more, Duchamp seemed to spend his time playing chess. He had learned the game as a child and had taken it up again with a passion during the War, when he was in Buenos Aires. Now he studied it day and night, and competed in many tournaments where he generally managed to do considerably better than break even. During the 1930s, in fact, Duchamp several times represented his country as a member of the French championship chess team.

Duchamp's relation to Surrealism was even more equivocal than his relation to Dada had been. None of his own paintings could be considered even peripherally Surrealist; there was never anything unconscious or "automatic" about Duchamp's creations. At the same time, his iconoclasm toward art and life was tremendously admired by all the Surrealists, and his abrupt termination of what would assuredly have been a brilliant career was decidedly impressive. The Surrealists often said that life had to be lived, not painted, and Duchamp, of all artists the most subtly subversive, had gone further than anyone else by acting on that assumption. Duchamp's reputation might not have endured as it did, though, if it had not been for André Breton's tireless championship. Breton, who would later describe Duchamp as "the most intelligent, and (for many) the most troublesome man of this first part of the 20th Century," was willing to accept Duchamp's independence of the movement for the same reason that he could accept Picasso's—because he valued so highly what each man had come to represent. It is even possible that Breton may have sensed in Duchamp the quality that was so totally lacking in himself: the saving sanity of humor. The absence of this quality was in part responsible for the factional struggles that beset the movement during the last half of the '20s, and it may also have contributed to the fatal imbalance that eventually led René Crevel, Jacques Rigaut, Oscar Dominguez and several other Surrealists to commit suicide, Antonin Artaud to go mad, and Yves Tanguy to take to alcohol and drugs. In the mid-'20s, though, the Surrealist dilemma was not psychological but political.

One of the last formal outbursts of Dada was a motion picture called *Entr'acte,* which was shown during the intermission of the ballet *Relâche.* The sequence shown here is from a scene in which Duchamp and Man Ray are playing chess on a rooftop when a torrent of water cascades down upon them, scattering the pieces and drenching the actors. Directed by René Clair, the film also featured as actors Picabia and Erik Satie, who composed the musical score.

Ever since 1925, Breton and his followers had been in constant disagreement over the issue of Surrealism's relations with the Communist Party. The "revolution in consciousness" had felt a natural affinity for Marxist ideology. Proclaiming that in order to "change life" it was necessary also to change the living conditions of the entire world, Breton had led the movement into a rather shaky popular front with the Communists, but he insisted on retaining Surrealist freedom of thought. It was possible, he maintained, to be Surrealist "first" and still to support the cause of social and economic revolution. His reasoning failed to impress the Communists either in France or Moscow and it provoked increasing opposition among the Surrealists of two kinds—those who favored total commitment to Moscow and those who wanted no political alliances of any kind. The crisis came to a head in 1929. Enraged by the mounting dissension, Breton read most of the original members out of the movement. The expelled members struck back with a pamphlet savagely attacking Breton (it was ironically called *Un Cadavre,* the same title used by the Surrealists for their famous 1924 pamphlet attacking the French novelist Anatole France).

In his "Second Surrealist Manifesto," published soon after the great purge, Breton announced that henceforth Surrealism's course would be directed toward a "true and profound occultation"—i.e., that it would become increasingly private and hermetic. What Breton did not yet realize was that domination of the movement by literary men was at an end. From 1929 on, Surrealism would be the painters' province.

Odysseys in the Mind

The unconscious mind, as Freud discovered, is a rolling sea of buried memories, primordial drives and unthinkable desires. When it surges over into the conscious mind in fever hallucinations or vivid dreams, it can be far more real than everyday "reality"; at its extremes, the unleashed unconscious mind can create illusions of paralyzing horror or transcendent beauty. This is the twilight world which the school of art known as Surrealism—"super-realism"—seeks to explore.

Surrealism emerged as a unified movement in 1924. André Breton, its founder, was a young poet who had studied Freud and had served during the War as an army psychiatrist. It was his belief that no artist has total conscious control over his work, that the unconscious is a prime arbiter of subject matter and style. Thus, Breton explored the artistic ramifications of Freud's thinking. What would be the results, Breton asked, if a person deliberately abdicated conscious control over his artistic impulses? His approach, lulling the mind into a state of semiconsciousness and recording its ramblings, was at first meant to apply to writing; he did not fully recognize its implications in the field of painting until he came across the chilling work of Giorgio de Chirico, done a decade earlier (*opposite*). Other gifted young painters like Max Ernst, Yves Tanguy, René Magritte, Joan Miró and Salvador Dali, some of whom were refugees from Dada, were swiftly attracted by the limitless possibilities of Surrealism.

At 26, Giorgio de Chirico recaptured in paint the terror that he had felt as a sickly child whenever he was confronted by his father's brutish masculinity. The eyes are closed, said one critic, "because had they been open he would not have dared to look."

Giorgio de Chirico: *The Child's Brain*, 1914

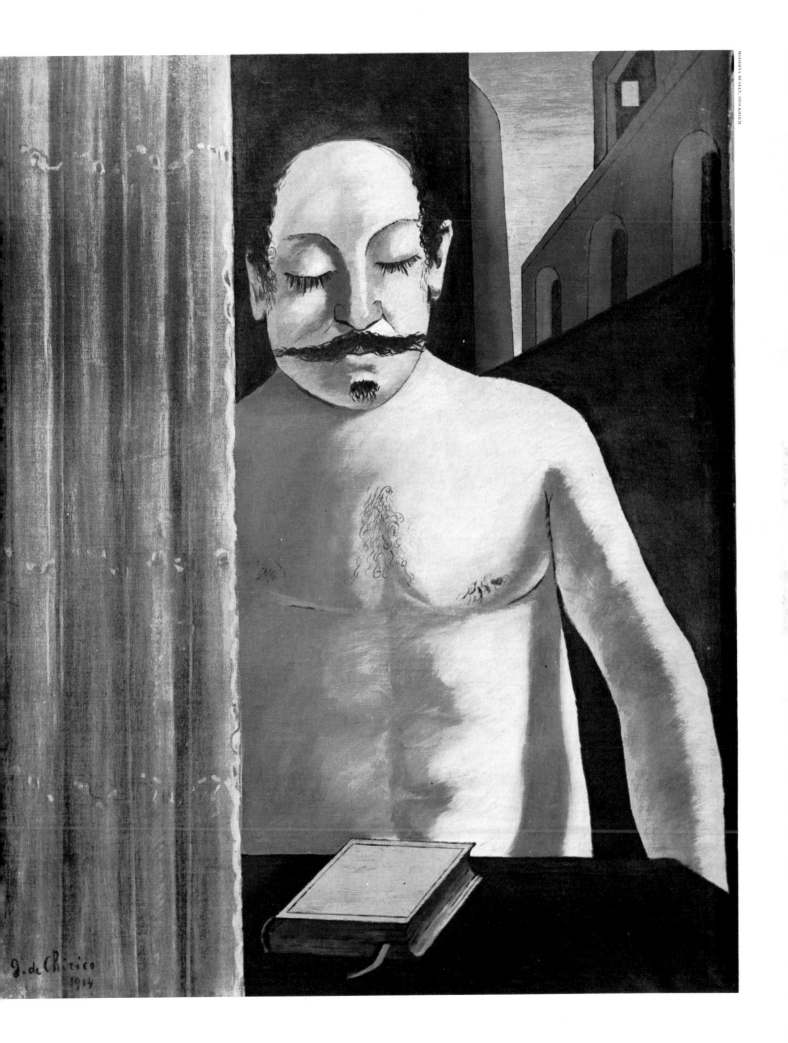

je ne vois pas la

cachée dans la forêt

Photo-montage created for *La Révolution Surréaliste, No. 12*, December 15, 1929.

Clockwise from top left: Maxime Alexandre, Louis Aragon, André Breton, Luis Buñuel, Jean Caupenne, Paul Eluard, Marcel Fourrier, René Magritte, Albert Valentin, André Thirion, Yves Tanguy, Georges Sadoul, Paul Nougé, Camille Goemans, Max Ernst, Salvador Dali. The painting in the center is by René Magritte.

Once they had established their group identity and their goal, the Surrealists, like all revolutionaries, tended to huddle together. They had their private jokes, and produced a number of joint works. One such is the magazine illustration at left, which shows 16 of them photographed with their eyes shut, surrounding a nude girl bearing the legend: "I do not see the [nude] hidden in the forest." This effort is thought by some to be a comment on de Chirico's painting of the man shown on the previous page, but the connection is cryptic and the humor long gone.

Such "in" jokes were typical of Surrealist output of the time. Others were Man Ray's acidulous turning of an Ingres-like nude into a violin (below), and a far-out film (right) featuring a man wiping his mouth from his face, a pair of trussed-up priests, a rotting donkey on a grand piano, and a human hand dripping with live ants.

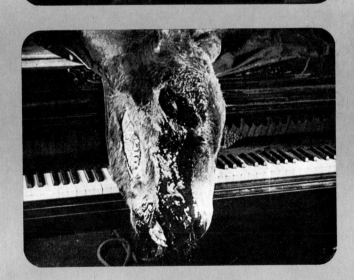

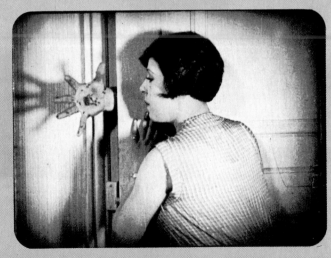

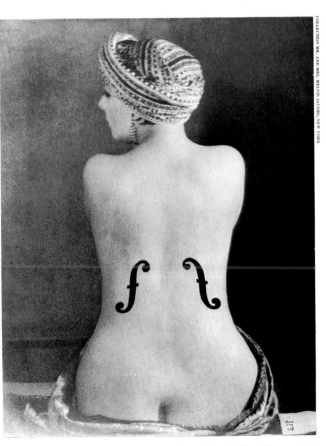

Man Ray: *Violon d'Ingres*, 1924

Salvador Dali and Luis Buñuel: Scenes from
Un Chien Andalou, 1929

Most avant-garde art movements blaze new trails; Surrealism was also able to find ancestors in the past. One inspiration was the Flemish painter Hieronymus Bosch, who created fantasy worlds containing both Garden-of-Eden delights *(right)* and the blackest horrors of Hell. Bosch was particularly interesting to the Surrealists because his pictures can be approached in several ways. At one level, they are Christian allegories; at another, they are stuffed with remarkable psychological symbols of a society wracked by devastating plagues and the terrors of the Inquisition.

The visual pun that so delighted the Surrealists goes back at least as far as 16th Century Italy, where a number of painters produced landscapes like the one below; tipped up so the left side is at the bottom, it becomes a monstrous face. Such multiple-image devices were revived by Salvador Dali.

A more immediate precursor of Surrealism was Odilon Redon, a French 19th Century painter who produced totally unreal images out of his unconscious *(left)*. "Nothing in art is achieved by will alone," he wrote in 1898. "Everything is done by docilely submitting to the unconscious."

Odilon Redon: *Winged Head above the Waters*, c. 1875

Merian: *Landscape-Head*, undated

Hieronymus Bosch (c. 1450-1516): *Garden of Delights*, d

Giorgio de Chirico: *The Soothsayer's Recompense*, 1913

Giorgio de Chirico's unsettling paintings, with their deep, brooding shadows, their distorted perspectives and their enigmatic subject matter, had a profound influence on the Surrealists. But he never actually joined the Surrealist clique and later went so far as to renounce the style, and even to claim that he had not painted pictures that were known to be by him.

Where can one look for the meaning of de Chirico's work? There are a few clues in his own life. His father, the naked figure with the closed eyes shown on page 109, was a railroad man. Does the train speeding through the bleak landscape in *The Soothsayer's Recompense (above)* also refer to him? What about that lonely tower in *Nostalgia of the Infinite?* It recalls a tower in Turin which de Chirico knew as a boy. The castle seen in the background of *The Disquieting Muses* is a familiar sight in

Giorgio de Chirico: *The Mystery and Melancholy of a Street*, 1914

Giorgio de Chirico: *Nostalgia of the Infinite*, probably 1913-14

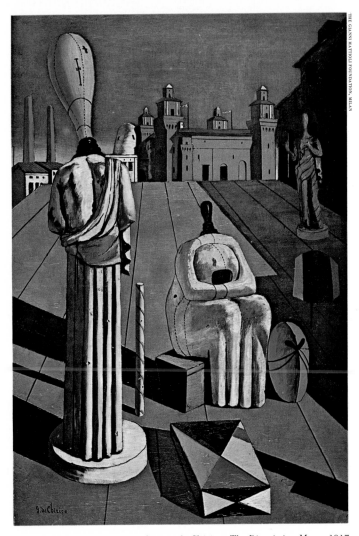

Ferrara. De Chirico was a remote man, and his colonnaded streets are still and empty, with only a small figure or two in them. Each is a depersonalized image: a reclining antique statue, a stitched leather head on a column, or a figure shown only in silhouette, like the little girl rolling her hoop toward a cryptic rendezvous with a shadowy figure, whose real being and mysterious purpose lie outside the frame of the picture entirely.

Giorgio de Chirico: *The Disquieting Muses*, 1917

Max Ernst's involvement with Surrealism apparently began as a child, when he experienced fevered visions during an attack of measles. Later, he found that he could induce similar hallucinations by staring fixedly at woodwork, clouds or any textured surface. Ernst's intense imagination, his ability to concentrate his vision and what he describes as his favorite occupation—"looking"— combine in his work to produce fascinatingly disoriented

Max Ernst: *Elephant of the Celebes,* 1921

images. In *Elephant of the Celebes (left)*, fish float in the air, bull's horns appear on the end of the elephant's pipelike trunk, and a headless plaster torso beckons. In *Two Children Are Threatened by a Nightingale (below)*, a gate swings from the canvas, where ghostly figures appear. Ernst admitted that the imagery may have stemmed from his childhood when a pet cockatoo died; he suffered for years from "a dangerous confusion between birds and humans."

Max Ernst: *Two Children Are Threatened by a Nightingale*, 1924

Yves Tanguy: *Dame à l'Absence*, 1942

De Chirico's elongated shadows and dramatic perspectives find an echo in the work of Frenchman Yves Tanguy, who saw one of de Chirico's paintings in the mid-1920s and is said to have become a Surrealist on the spot. Unlike his inspirer, Tanguy was not content to explore the enigmas of ordinary objects but preferred to create his own. At first he painted pictures like *The Storm (right)*, with recognizable elements. The painting does look stormy, there are clouds, something that could be a wave-dashed lighthouse, and a suggestion of undersea life. But Tanguy's subject matter became more unreal. There are no familiar objects in the pictures below, though they are painted with great precision. Tanguy's later work emphasizes flat landscapes filled with objects of complexity like the clifflike form at left (executed after he came to America in 1939). All of his paintings have elements of the unexpected. As he puts it: "I found that if I planned a picture beforehand, it never surprised me, and surprises are my pleasure in painting."

Yves Tanguy: *The Storm*, 1926

Yves Tanguy: *Mama, Papa is Wounded!*, 1927

Yves Tanguy: *Parallels*, 1929

Paul Delvaux: *The Break of Day*, 1937

Some of the most striking Surrealist works are those in which perfectly natural elements are presented in wildly unnatural ways to startle or disorient the viewer. Paul Delvaux is famous for the buxom nudes that wander in broad daylight (or moonlight) through his paintings like sleepwalkers or, as in the painting above, are permanently rooted in the earth as tree-women.

René Magritte used the same surprise technique, but in a more humorous and philosophical vein. "When a man thinks about the moon," he said of the three moons at right, "it becomes *his* moon." And of the immense rock in the air *(far right)* he said, "In thinking the stone must fall, the viewer has a greater sentiment of what a stone is than if the stone is on the ground."

René Magritte: *The Masterpiece or the Mysteries of the Horizon*, 1955

120

René Magritte: *Château des Pyrénées*, 1959

VI

Limp Watches
and High Ideals

Beauty will be convulsive *or will not be at all.* —ANDRE BRETON

In Surrealism's first decade, great stress was placed on the anonymous or collective nature of the works produced by automatic methods. Max Ernst even claimed that Surrealism had abolished the concept of talent. Surrealist painting, he said, "is within the reach of everybody who is attracted by real revelations and is therefore ready to assist inspiration and make it work to order." A Surrealist artist was to be judged not by the degree of technical skill he demonstrated but rather by the success with which he evoked unconscious material, and any method was theoretically as valid as any other.

By the time of the 1929 crisis, though, two separate and distinct techniques had emerged in Surrealist painting. In one, which derived from Giorgio de Chirico and was exemplified in the work of Magritte, a meticulous realism was applied to fantastic objects, or to familiar objects placed in surroundings so unusual that they became fantastically disoriented. In the other, developed mainly by Ernst and Masson, the artist sought by spontaneous or automatic methods to evoke, rather than to illustrate, the buried unconscious imagery. Each of these tendencies would henceforth be carried to much greater lengths by Salvador Dali and Joan Miró, two young artists who had almost nothing in common with one another except their place of origin: both were Spaniards, from Catalonia. Neither Dali nor Miró stayed for very long within the confines of the official Surrealist movement. Their mature styles were formed by their contact with Surrealism, however, and for decades they, along with Ernst, were its most widely known exponents.

It is still too early to assess Dali's position in modern art. Dali himself so muddied the waters by his calculated eccentricities, his tireless self-publicity, his pseudo-philosophies and his obvious courtship of high society and money—to say nothing at all of much meretricious painting—that the brilliance of his early work is often overlooked by critics and by his fellow artists, most of whom look upon him with utter contempt. In 1929, though, Dali's spectacular appearance on the scene electrified the Paris Surrealists and gave rise to the most exaggerated hopes. "With the coming of Dali," Breton wrote in 1929, "it is perhaps the

One of 23 paintings in his "Constellation" series, this work reveals Joan Miró at his most lyrical. The violence that haunted some of his earlier work has been replaced by joyous symbols and exquisitely balanced shapes.

Joan Miró: *The Beautiful Bird Revealing the Unknown to a Pair of Lovers,* July 23, 1941

123

first time that the mental windows have been opened really wide, so that one can feel oneself gliding up toward the wild sky's trap." Although he had certain reservations about Dali even then, Breton was inclined to believe that Surrealism had at last found its native genius.

For his own part, Dali could claim with justification that he had been a Surrealist since birth. He was born on May 11, 1904, in the town of Figueras, near Barcelona. The son of a notary (like Duchamp), he grew up in comfortable surroundings and learned very quickly how to impose his tyrannical will on those around him. Three years before he was born, an older brother had died of meningitis, and Dali, who received the same Christian name, was seldom denied anything by his doting, anxious parents. As he described it in his autobiography, *The Secret Life of Salvador Dali*, his childhood was marked by hysterical and often violent incidents—Dali slashing his favorite nurse with a safety pin, gratuitously pushing a small playmate off a bridge, flinging himself down a stone staircase to astonish his schoolmates. An altogether extraordinary imagination obliged him, even as a child, to consider himself a genius, and "if you play at genius," Dali said, "you become one." His ego has surmounted all obstacles since then with dazzling virtuosity. "I was destined, as my name indicates, for nothing less than to rescue painting from the void of modern art," he would write, "and to do so in this abominable epoch of mechanical and mediocre catastrophes in which we have the distress and the dishonor to live."

Dali's altered *Mona Lisa*, which shows his own face and a pair of hairy hands filled with coins, is a takeoff on the earlier Duchamp transfiguration of the masterpiece *(page 61)*. Asked what he thought of the Leonardo original, Dali replied evasively, "I am a very great admirer of Marcel Duchamp, who happens to be the man who has made those famous transformations on the face of the Gioconda. He drew a very small mustache on her, a mustache that was already Dalinian."

Dali's technical gifts as an artist were clearly evident from the start. By the time he was 17, when he entered the School of Fine Arts in Madrid—from which he would later be expelled for refusing to take exams from professors whom he denounced as intellectual inferiors—he had already experimented fluently with almost every modern style from Impressionism to Cubism. He had also developed a passionate interest in some of the old masters, notably Vermeer, as well as a lifelong obsession with the work of Picasso. He soon decided that the Madrid instructors had nothing to teach him. When his class was told to copy a Gothic statue of the Virgin, Dali infuriated the teacher by carefully drawing a pair of scales. "Perhaps you see a Virgin like everyone else," Dali said haughtily, "but I see a pair of scales." The incident was significant in view of his later Surrealist theories. Dali, however, did not discover his true direction as an artist for several more years. With incredible virtuosity he continued to master and discard one style after another, including the *scuola metafisica* of de Chirico and Carrà, until he came to Paris in 1928 and discovered Surrealism.

It was Miró who first introduced Dali to the Surrealists, and for a while after that Dali's painting showed the influence of his fellow Catalonian. By the summer of 1929, though, he had started to work on a small canvas whose minutely detailed, irrational images—animals, insects, bits of human anatomy, a statue with an enormously enlarged hand—were copied as closely as possible from specific dreams: it was what Dali would later call a "hand-painted dream photograph." A group of Surrealists including Paul Eluard and his wife Gala, René and Georgette Margritte, and the dealer Camille Goemans came down that same summer to Cadaqués, the little fishing village near Figueras where Dali was living at the time, and it was Eluard who gave the painting its title—*The Lugubrious Game*. He was to contribute more than that, as it turned out. Dali fell madly in love with Gala Eluard, the Russian-born girl who had so fascinated Max Ernst a few years before. Gala felt strongly attracted to Dali in spite of his strange behavior; at this period he was subject to fits of hysterical laughter so violent that he felt he was in danger of going mad. It was Gala, he believed, who drew him back from the edge of madness that summer. She left Eluard the following year to live with Dali, and they were married soon afterward. Since then he has never tired of publicly worshiping at her shrine.

Dali had his first one-man show in Paris in November 1929, at the Galerie Goemans. Just a month before, the Paris intelligentsia had attended the première of a sensational film made by Dali and Luis Buñuel, whom Dali had met when he was at the Madrid School of Fine Arts. The film, which was called *Un Chien Andalou (An Andalusian Dog)*, opened with a closeup of a woman's eyeball being sliced by a razor, and reached its Surrealist climax with a scene that showed a man struggling at the end of a long rope that was attached to two grand pianos, over which were draped the bloody, mud-caked carcasses of two dead donkeys. As a result of the film and his one-man show, Dali was suddenly catapulted into prominence as Surrealism's man of the hour. Breton wrote a glowing preface for the exhibition at Goemans, but prophetically added a note of warning: "Dali is like a man who hesitates between talent and genius, or, as one would have said in a previous age, between vice and virtue. . . . On one side there are the mites which attempt to cling to his clothes and never leave him even when he goes out on the street. . . . On the other side there is hope; the hope that everything will not crash into ruins after all and that, to start with, the sound of Dali's admirable voice may continue to ring true in his own ears, despite the interest that certain 'materialists' have in persuading him to confuse it with the creaking of his patent-leather shoes."

The paintings that Dali executed in the years from 1929 to 1934 are, with a very few others from later periods, the ones on which his future reputation will undoubtedly rest. Many of them are surprisingly small. *Accommodations of Desire (page 139)* is only a little more than 8 by 13 inches; *Illumined Pleasures* is about the same size, and *The Persistence of Memory (page 139)*, the most famous of all, is 10 inches by 14. Within this limited space, Dali achieved effects of the greatest intensity. Borrowing from de Chirico the technique of elongated shadows and abruptly scaled-down perspective, he projected with startling clarity the obsessions and erotic fetishes of his own subconscious: shoes, keys, women's hair, decaying flesh, snarling lions, fried eggs, madwomen with idiot grins, swarming ants and the well-known limp watches.

Dali had a great deal to say about the recurrent images that appear in his work. Some of his statements are pure buffoonery (the important thing about limp watches, he says, is that "they keep good time"), but his autobiography reveals the origin of most of them in specific experiences of his vivid childhood. The temptation to psychoanalyze Dali

Among Dali's many curious preoccupations is a rather strange interest in his brother, who died before Dali was born. In *Portrait of My Dead Brother* above, Dali rendered the image with small, round dots, which merge to form the brother's face. This technique is used in Pop Art.

from his paintings is almost irresistible—the fear of impotence in those limp watches and soft, useless appendages supported by crutches; the anxiety in his obsession with the praying mantis, an insect species whose female member has the regrettable trait of devouring the male immediately following copulation. Dali never objected to this interpretation, and certainly no artist has profited more than he from the discoveries of Freud. Dali did more than put his neuroses to work on canvas, however; he contributed to Surrealism an entirely new method of forcing inspiration, based on the deliberate exploitation of the mental derangement called paranoia.

The Surrealists were all fascinated by the phenomenon of insanity. Their attitude toward it somewhat resembled the attitude of those primitive societies that looked upon an insane person as one divinely inspired. Seeking as they did the deliberate "derangement of all the senses" recommended by Rimbaud, the Surrealists studied the drawings and writings of the insane in search of keys to their own kingdom of desire, and even courted insanity in their private lives—Breton's beautiful and strangely moving book *Nadja*, for example, is an account of his long love affair with a deranged girl who ended in an institution. Dali claimed absolute pre-eminence in this domain, boasting that "The only difference between a madman and myself is that I am not mad." His particular "talent," he said, lay in the realm of paranoia, in which the madman substitutes for reality his own delusions and hallucinations.

In 1930 Dali published a book called *La Femme Visible* wherein he described the method of Surrealist painting that he had discovered, which he called the "paranoiac-critical method." Simply stated, it was the deliberate substitution of Dalinian hallucination for observed reality. Dali had practiced it years before in art school, when he drew the pair of scales in place of the Virgin; he claimed that his sensitivity gave him the power to substitute delusion for reality at will, and he made it clear that he considered this "active" method of forcing inspiration superior to the "passive" techniques of automatism and dream transcription.

Dali's own paranoiac-critical activity was especially apparent in his use of double and multiple images. Although many artists have used this trick—Arcimboldo in the 16th Century painted landscapes that turned into heads, and Currier and Ives popularized puzzle pictures containing hidden images—none has ever used it more skillfully than Dali. He believes that paranoiacs have a particular ability to see more than one "reality" in any given scene, and such is Dali's extraordinary gift that he not only perceives these alternate realities but makes the viewer see them as well. In *The Invisible Man (page 141)*, the "paranoiac" image is a seated nude male figure extending from top to bottom of the picture. In *Nostalgic Echo*, the figure of a girl skipping rope is repeated exactly by the image of a bell in a church tower. Sometimes the double image becomes overly insistent, as in the 1938 *Apparition of Face and Fruit-Dish on a Beach*, but at his best Dali paints so deceptively that the second image appears only after careful study, and then with such truly paranoiac force that the viewer can see nothing else.

Dali was so pleased with his paranoiac-critical method that he applied it in a variety of different ways, often with the most surprising results. Through paranoia-criticism, he "discovered" that Millet's well-known 19th Century painting *The Angelus*, which showed a peasant couple standing in a field, their heads bent in pious devotion, contained a hidden wealth of sexual symbolism. According to Dali, this was the real reason for the painting's great popularity. He painted a series of variations on the sexual "themes" of *The Angelus*, and another series based on the literary legend of William Tell, whose real theme he had ascertained to be cannibalistic: the father wanted to eat his son. Dali, of course, was out to shock and provoke the public in every way possible. He realized this ambition with notable success during the brief run in 1930 of *L'Age d'Or*, his second film with Buñuel. *L'Age d'Or* contained scenes that showed a dog being squashed to death, a father killing his son and a closeup of the heroine ecstatically sucking the big toe of a statue of Apollo; the film ended with a shot of several women's scalps nailed to a crucifix. Showings of *L'Age d'Or* at Studio 28 in Paris were abruptly terminated when a band of young toughs from the protofascist Camelots du Roi organization invaded the theater, hurled ink at the screen, attacked the audience and destroyed an exhibition of paintings by Miró, Ernst, Dali and Tanguy in the lobby.

When Dali settled in Paris in 1929 he had been content at first to play a relatively docile role in the Surrealist movement, accepting Breton's authority and confining his eccentricities to such minor matters as his habit of paying for drinks with a 100-franc note—he could not be bothered, he maintained, with bills of smaller denomination. He embraced all the necessary Surrealist beliefs and dutifully renounced his own family, his country and the Catholic Church. As Dali's fame grew, however, his natural self-esteem began to assert itself more and more. He openly proclaimed the superiority of paranoia-criticism to previous Surrealist techniques. He peremptorily decided to eulogize Jean Louis Ernest Meissonier, the 19th Century academic realist, and tried hard to have him formally anointed as a Surrealist precursor. This sort of thing led to increasing friction with Breton, who still admired Dali's painting but who did nothing to conceal his distaste for some of Dali's ideas. The situation reached a crisis in 1934, over the issue of politics. The rise of Hitler had pushed the Surrealists into one last attempt to make common cause with the Communists, an attempt that was doomed to failure but in which Dali took no part. Hitler, meanwhile, had made surprising and incomprehensible appearances in two paintings by Dali. Breton called a meeting of the Surrealist group in his Rue Fontaine studio, and summoned Dali to come and account for his political views. Dali arrived with a thermometer in his mouth. Claiming that he had the flu, he kept it there throughout the proceedings, taking it out from time to time to read his temperature. Despite this impediment he argued his case with extreme vehemence. Dali insisted that as a true Surrealist he had the obligation to transcribe his dreams without interference from his conscious mind, and that it was not his fault if he happened to dream of Hitler. Several times he knelt down at Breton's feet, "not to plead against being ex-

Like artist-goldsmiths of the Renaissance, Dali designed works of art using gold and precious stones. Few of his designs are functional, although the *Eye of Time* (*top*) is a watch. *Ruby Lips* is more characteristic: here Dali takes literally the romantic cliché of "lips like rubies and teeth like pearls."

pelled," he has written, "but, on the contrary, to exhort Breton to understand that my obsession with Hitler was strictly paranoid and essentially apolitical." What actually happened after that is still not clear. Some say Dali was expelled; Dali maintains that he was not. In any case, Dali had reached a point where he no longer required the support of the Surrealists.

His exhibition in June 1934 at the Galerie Jacques Bonjean had established him as a complete success with the critics and the Parisian *haut monde*, and Dali, for his part, had discovered that the world of international society was "infinitely more vulnerable to my system of ideas than the artists." He would henceforth exploit this discovery by every possible means, and nowhere more successfully than in America.

The American dealer Julien Levy, who introduced Surrealist painting in the United States, had bought Dali's *Persistence of Memory*, which was subsequently acquired by The Museum of Modern Art in New York. With its melting watches and jewel-like ants, this picture soon established itself as the key work of Surrealism in America, and when Dali came to New York for the first time in 1934 his flamboyant antics accordingly received close attention. Surrealism by this time had become chic. Fashionable women reflected the new fad in their clothing and their hats and even in the decoration of their rooms, and everything that was absurd or wittily outrageous became "surrealistic." Dali threw himself with gusto into the commercialization of the movement—designing clothes for Schiaparelli, decorating windows for Bonwit Teller (and then shattering the store window when his mannequins were changed), making fantastic statements to the press at every opportunity. When Levy planned a Surrealist exhibit at the 1939 New York World's Fair, his financial backers, dazzled by Dali, overruled Levy's arrangement with other artists so that Dali could install his own "Dream of Venus" show instead. Dali maintained that he *was* Surrealism, and a good many wealthy and influential people agreed with him.

He could still produce extraordinary work. Dali's 1936 *Soft Construction with Boiled Beans: Premonition of Civil War (page 140)*, now in the Philadelphia Museum, is in its own way as powerful as The Museum of Modern Art's gigantic *Guernica*, the painting with which Picasso expressed his anguish and rage over the conflict that was rending their native Spain. Dali, however, gave verbal support to the Franco side in the Spanish Civil War; Julien Levy wondered at the time if Dali may not have done so out of his unadmitted sense of rivalry with Picasso, who supported the Republican cause. When many of the Surrealists came to America after the fall of France in 1940, they would have nothing to do with Dali, whom Breton had scornfully rechristened with the anagram "Avida Dollars." Only Duchamp continued to see him, but Duchamp had remained aloof from politics as well as art, and not even Breton could prevent him from indulging his interest in Dali as one of the great egotists of the age.

Since that time, although Dali's work has found favor with certain sectors of wealthy society and with a large public that appreciates his technical mastery and is pleasantly titillated by his erotic and vaguely "shocking" subject matter, it has been uniformly damned by critics and modern artists. Dali announced some time ago that he was going to "become classic" in the manner of his illustrious predecessors Raphael, Leonardo, Velázquez and Vermeer, and that it was his sacred duty to rescue art from the formless ugliness of modernism. His rediscovery of the Catholic Church resulted in a number of large and exceedingly vulgar pictures on traditional religious themes, brought up to date by a "nuclear mysticism" that atomizes the image into whirling fragments, or floats the subject melodramatically in mid-air.

In the years following 1950, during which he and Gala divided their time between winters at the St. Regis Hotel in New York and summers in the picturesque fishing village of Port Lligat, near his birthplace of Figueras, Dali's paintings tended to become larger, more crowded and less convincing than ever. It would appear that Breton's 1929 warning was prophetic indeed, and that the society "mites" that cling to his clothes finally made it impossible for Dali to distinguish his own voice from the creaking of his patent-leather shoes. This will not prevent his early work from being recognized in some quarters—and more widely in years to come—as an exceptionally brilliant, perhaps the most brilliant, contribution to Surrealist painting, and an achievement of considerable importance in the history of modern art. It is in these small, luminous, hallucinated paintings that the artist realized his pictorial ambition, which he once described as the ability "to materialize the images of concrete irrationality with the most imperialist fury of precision, in order that the world of the imagination and of concrete irrationality may be as objectively evident, of the same consistency, of the same durability, of the same persuasive, cognoscitive and communicative thickness as that of the exterior world of phenomenal reality." That is the unique, authentic, but no longer audible voice of Salvador Dali.

If Dali represents the quixotic aspect of the Spanish temper, Joan Miró can be seen as his exact antithesis. Miró inherited the Catalan peasant virtues of quiet perseverance and stubborn courage, and he retained, all his life, the miraculous vision of a child.

Joan Miró's grandfather had been a country blacksmith. His father was a watchmaker and goldsmith, a highly respected craftsman in the old section of Barcelona, where Miró was born in 1893. He seemed a thoroughly ordinary child: obedient, dutiful, untalented. A poor student, he showed an early and absorbing interest in drawing, which he practiced at every opportunity, but with uninspired results. "I was a marvel of clumsiness," Miró once said of his student efforts. After three years of attending a commercial trade school and taking art classes, Miró went to work as a bookkeeper. The following year he suffered one of those blows of fate by which artists are sometimes formed. Miró's health broke down in 1911, and he was forced to spend the next half year recuperating in the country, at a farm his parents had just bought near the village of Montroig. Here he not only regained his health but drew from the sun-drenched landscape the strength that would never cease to flow forth into his art.

For the next three years Miró studied at Francisco Galí's private art school in Barcelona. Having persuaded his parents that art was the only career possible for him, he still had serious doubts about his own ability. "I lack all plastic means with which to express myself," he confessed to a friend in 1915, "and I feel rotten about it. Sometimes I knock my head against the wall in despair." Gradually, though, he mastered the elements of plastic expression and began to attract more notice as a promising young Catalan painter. A series of portraits and still lifes of this period show Miró's major influences: Cézanne and Van Gogh, the Fauves, Cubism. At the same time, in his distortions and simplifications of form, and in his fresh, bold handling of color he gave unmistakable evidence of his own emerging style, a style that announced itself distinctly in the landscapes of Montroig that he painted during the summer months. Miró's feeling for nature was so intense and yet so intimate that during this period he never subordinated details to the total effect, preferring instead to paint each element with meticulous and equal devotion. "What I am interested in most of all," he wrote to a fellow artist, "is the calligraphy of a tree or the tiles of a roof, leaf by leaf, twig by twig, blade by blade of grass." The trees, fields, farmhouses, animals and sky of Montroig are the recurrent images in these early "detailist" paintings, which reached their culmination in Miró's first masterpiece, *The Farm (page 144)*.

T*he Farm* was begun in Montroig in the summer of 1921 but it was finished in Paris, where Miró, feeling a need to touch the springs of modern art, had been spending his winters since 1919. Miró worked on it constantly for nine months, with such a passion for authenticity that when he left Montroig for Paris he took along two sample tufts of grass to refer to as models. When the painting was finished it hung for a while in a Montparnasse café, and was eventually bought by a virtually penniless young American writer named Ernest Hemingway, who earned the money to pay for it by loading and unloading sacks of vegetables every night at Les Halles, the Paris produce market. "No one could look at it and not know it had been painted by a great painter," Hemingway once wrote. "It has in it all that you feel about Spain when you are there and all that you feel when you are away and cannot go there." With its combination of childlike spontaneity and stylized organization, its near-perfect blending of fact and fantasy, its formal solidity and pure, scintillating color, *The Farm* is not only a synthesis of all that Miró had learned thus far but a point of reference for the future—the key, in effect, to his entire career.

The next big step left realism behind. The progression can be seen most clearly by a comparison of *The Farm* with *The Tilled Field*, which Miró painted one year later. *The Tilled Field* has almost all the same elements as the earlier canvas. Here again are the trees, the farmhouse, the road, the farm animals, the lizard, the snail—but everything has become transformed by fantasy. The pine tree at the right has an ear growing from its trunk, and its branches frame an enormous eye. The fig tree is purely schematic, with only a single leaf and fig at the tip of one branch to identify it. The animals, painted with the same painstaking detail as before, have became fabulous and mythological. Perspective is almost eliminated; the colors are wholly arbitrary, and so are the individual proportions—the snail is as large as the dog.

All these tendencies were soon to be carried a great deal further. In *Catalan Landscape (page 145)*, which Miró finished in 1924, we find much greater schematization of detail—some forms have become geometrical spheres, triangles, squares or cones; others have become straight lines, curlicues or dotted curves. *Maternity* shows the same method applied to a simple composition of a woman nursing her two children; the mother's head is a sort of black helmet sprouting long hairs; her body is a straight line that ends in a heavy black triangle with a rounded bottom; at either end of another straight line that intersects the body are her two breasts, one a white circle from which hangs the girl child, the other, seen in profile, a black half-circle supporting the boy. A red-and-yellow, wormlike form represents the woman's inner organs. In *Harlequin's Carnival*, Miró has filled a room with fantasy figures of every description, including the "escape ladder" that is to figure in many of his future works. The mood of these paintings is whimsical, humorous, brilliantly colorful and hugely animated, but Miró's intention was by no means frivolous. Far from trying to escape from reality, he sought to "escape into the absolute of nature"—an absolute that included imagination and fantasy as well as fact. "Hard at work and full of enthusiasm," he wrote to his friend J. F. Rafols while working on *Catalan Landscape*. "Monstrous animals and angelic animals. Trees with ears and a peasant in a Catalan cap, holding a shotgun and smoking a pipe. All the pictorial problems solved. To express with precision all the golden sparks the soul gives off."

Miró's preoccupations at this moment were very close to those of the Surrealists, with whom he was already on good terms. Although the first person he had called on when he arrived in Paris was Picasso (who received him warmly and even bought one of his paintings, a self-portrait), Miró never succumbed to the powerful attraction of his slightly older countryman's art. He soon met André Masson and, through him, the rest of the Surrealist group, and during the 1920s his best friends were the Surrealist poets. Miró had discovered Rimbaud, Mallarmé and Alfred Jarry on his own, and it was his frequently stated ambition to make his art "attain poetry." His contact with Breton, Eluard and others reinforced his own natural inclination to pursue his fantasies and to seek out the marvelous. Miró joined the movement soon after its official founding in 1924, and he exhibited in group shows with the Surrealists for many years. It is important nevertheless to recognize that with his quiet, rather shy personality, he was never a very active member of the group. He seldom attended meetings or went to the right bank Café Cyrano, where the Surrealists gathered in those days. Miró's only recorded Surrealist action took place during the height of the Surrealist experiments in Paris, when it was decided that each member would carry out some form of public provocation. Robert Desnos, for example, said "*Bonjour, madame,*" to a priest on the subway. Michel Leiris insulted a gendarme, and kept on doing so all the

Like his paintings, Miró's sculptures are
characterized by great freedom of form and
playful fantasy. The one above, called *Objet
Poétique*, is a construction of found
objects, among which are a hat, a toy fish,
a doll's leg, a map and a stuffed parrot.
In Miró's sculptures of this kind, the
items are selected at random and assembled
spontaneously in a spirit of burlesque.

way to the police station, where he was held for 48 hours. Paul Eluard
walked around a public square shouting, "Down with the Army! Down
with France!" until he, too, landed in jail. Miró, who was also expect-
ed to commit some outrage, went out on the street one day and began
saying, rather politely, "Down with the Mediterranean!" The other
Surrealists were disgusted, but Miró argued that, because the Mediterranean was the cradle of Western culture, what he had really been saying was, "Down with everything."

Aside from the short-lived excommunication of Miró and Max Ernst
for their 1926 collaboration with Diaghilev, no one sought to force the
Surrealists' rigid group discipline on Miró. Breton even acknowledged,
once, that "Miró may rank as the most Surrealist of us all."

The whole Surrealist group turned out for the opening of Miró's
second Paris exhibition, at the Galerie Pierre in 1925, and so did nearly
everyone else in the Paris avant-garde. Jacques Viot, the show's or-
ganizer, has provided a description of the great night: "The paintings
on the wall dumfounded those who could get a look at them. But I
think that the artist amazed even more because nobody could figure out
any connection between his works and his person. Miró made an enormous effort to make himself attractive. . . . He wore an embroidered
waistcoat, gray trousers, and white spats. He was profuse in paying
compliments, but so afraid he might overlook somebody that he almost
gave an impression of anxiety. When it was over, we persuaded him to
go up to Montmartre with us, and I have a very clear recollection of
Miró, looking more preoccupied than ever, dancing a tango with a
woman much taller than he. Not once did he slip—not a single step or
a tiny gesture was omitted. The other dancers stopped, unable to com-
pete with such conscientiousness. And Miró, all tensed up, kept right
on doing the tango as though he had just learned it out of a book."

Encouraged by the Surrealists but responsive only to his own inner
voice, Miró now crossed, in Breton's phrase, "the final barriers re-
straining him from total spontaneity of expression." During the years
1925, 1926 and 1927 Miró painted more than a hundred pictures in
which he was no longer dealing with familiar objects fancifully treated,
but with almost wholly abstract dream imagery. His method was close
to automatism. He worked in a kind of creative frenzy that was often
intensified by hunger, for in spite of his success with the avant-garde
his work sold poorly and he could seldom afford to eat more than one
meal a day. Some of these works clearly foreshadow the American Abstract Expressionist painting of the 1940s. Applying his color in thin
washes and allowing it to drip down the canvas, painting so rapidly that
the gesture, the act itself, became the subject, Miró was not illustrating his dreams as Dali did, but rather re-creating the dream experience.
In several pictures, written words enter and help to form the image.
The biomorphic shapes that appear are sometimes reminiscent of the
forms used by Jean Arp, whom Miró saw often during this period (they
had taken studios in the same Montmartre block with Max Ernst and
René Magritte), although Arp denied that Miró was influenced by him.

Miró had also come to admire the work of Paul Klee, which may have had some effect on the more humorous canvases that he painted in the course of his summer sojourns in Montroig during this period. These paintings have become better known than the others he did in the mid-'20s, and they are certainly among his more delightful productions in the earlier vein of playful fantasy. Two of the most famous are now in America: *Person Throwing a Stone at a Bird* in The Museum of Modern Art shows a figure that consists principally of one huge foot, with a straight line for the body and another for the arms, from the end of which a stone describes a precise but ineffectual arc toward a scarlet-crested bird; and *Dog Barking at the Moon (page 145)* in the Philadelphia Museum of Art, with its brown earth and black sky, its semihuman dog and its ladder linking earth and sky, reality and dream.

There is some cause for believing that Picasso himself may have been influenced by Miró's dream paintings. In 1927, Picasso turned from his formal abstractions to a new and disturbing style in which strange and menacing forms, monsters and chimeras made a direct assault upon the viewer's emotions. This is generally considered Picasso's Surrealist period, for although he never officially joined the movement, it was obvious that from 1927 to 1929 he was working in close alliance with Surrealism. Referring to this period Breton later wrote, "It can be said that Miró's influence . . . was to a large extent a determining one."

Like all organic things, Miró's art was continually evolving and changing. A trip to Holland in 1928 gave rise to the so-called "Dutch interiors," a series in which Miró subjected the intimate realism of paintings by Jan Steen and other Dutch 17th Century masters to elaborately fanciful distortions of all kinds. Soon afterward, assailed by doubts regarding the essential value of art, he set out, as he put it, "to wring the neck of painting." This sudden crisis in his development bore no apparent relation to his private life. At about the same time, in October of 1929, Miró married Pilar Juncosa, a Majorcan girl, and to his friends in Paris he seemed as cheerful as ever. Miró later intimated that his doubts were really a delayed reaction to Dadaism, which he had discovered first when, as a young art student in Barcelona in 1917, he met Picabia and read several issues of *391*, and which he later observed at first hand during the 1919 and 1920 Dada manifestations in Paris. In any case, Miró had abandoned his vibrant colors and animated forms and began to make Dadaist collages and constructions out of such unpainterly materials as string, linoleum, nails, scrap metal and junk of all kinds. His 1928 *Spanish Dancer* was simplicity itself: on a virgin canvas, a single feather, attached to a cork by a long hatpin.

Gradually, these rough "anti-art" productions gave way to large canvases in which the collage elements—sentimental postcards, butterflies, bits of newspaper advertising—served satiric or humorous ends. By 1932 he was no longer at war with painting. The 18 large pictures that he finished in 1933 are among the most magnificent of his entire career—serenely beautiful works such as The Museum of Modern Art's simply titled *Painting*, all of which proclaim Miró's absolute mastery of color and his spontaneous and childlike joy in painting. It was as

Léonide Massine, the great French ballet dancer and choreographer, was an early fan of Miró's, and in 1931, he asked the artist to design scenery and costumes for a new ballet *Jeux d'Enfants*. At the top above is Miró's sketch for the basic scene—a stylized comet's tail and a sphere—and some of the costumes. Movable painted panels, ornamented shields and animal heads completed the décor. The photograph at bottom shows the actual set during a performance, with a dancer's legs visible beneath the comet.

though, out of his struggle with doubt and uncertainty, Miró had won through to a complete freedom of expression. "Miró could not put a dot on a sheet of paper without hitting square on the target," said the sculptor Alberto Giacometti, at this time one of his closest friends. "He was so truly a painter that it was enough for him to drop three spots of color on the canvas, and it would come to life—it would be a painting." The simple, rhythmically flowing forms in these paintings of 1933 may appear to be abstract, but Miró has always vigorously denied being an abstractionist. "For me a form is never something abstract," he once said; "it is always a sign of something. It is always a man, a bird, or something else. For me painting is never form for form's sake."

His serenely joyful mood did not last. Like Picasso and a few other artists, Miró sensed and reflected in his art the approach of terrible events in the world around him. Beginning about 1934, his paintings were invaded by monsters, bestial forms whose features grew more and more grotesque and frightening. A brutal eroticism made its appearance: figures with huge, luridly colored genitals coupled with savage violence. Miró's color became feverish and almost unbearably intense. Even the titles of his pictures were alarming: *Personages in Front of a Volcano, Man and Woman in Front of a Heap of Excrement.* Miró had been spending an increasing amount of his time in Montroig and Barcelona since the birth of his daughter in 1931, but the outbreak of the Spanish Civil War forced him to leave his beloved Catalan countryside. Back in Paris, he could scarcely bring himself to paint. He enrolled in the Grande Chaumière academy and spent several months drawing from the figure, alongside art students 20 years younger than he was; Miró's nude studies show the female body so hideously distorted that it is almost unrecognizable. He worked for five months on *Still Life with an Old Shoe*, pouring into its realistic detail and melancholy color all his anguished feeling for the sufferings of his country.

His "wild paintings" reached a final peak of intensity with the 1938 *Seated Woman I* that is now in the Peggy Guggenheim Collection in Venice. Then, surprisingly, Miró turned his back on the approaching horrors. A group of exquisite small paintings on burlap that are among the most beautiful he had ever done was followed in 1939 by 23 miraculous gouaches, the "Constellations." Miró began work on this series while he was living in the village of Varengeville, in Normandy. Seemingly oblivious to the 1940 Nazi breakthrough on the Western front, he did not interrupt his work until the Wehrmacht was approaching Paris; then he somehow managed to get himself, his wife and daughter on the last train leaving for the Spanish border. They settled in Palma, Majorca, with his wife's family, and Miró completed the series there. The "Constellations," all done on the same size paper and in the same technique, are delicate, classically balanced works in which Miró's familiar "signs" for men, birds and stars combine with purely geometrical shapes in an atmosphere of perfect peace and serenity. Describing his state of mind when he painted them, Miró said, "I felt a deep desire to escape. I closed myself within myself purposely. The night, music, and the stars began to play a major role in suggesting my paintings. Music had always appealed to me, and now music in this period began to take the role poetry had played in the early twenties, especially Bach and Mozart." One of the finest of the "Constellation" series can be seen in The Museum of Modern Art, under the poetic title *The Beautiful Bird Revealing the Unknown to a Pair of Lovers (page 122)*.

After the War, Miró lived for the most part in Majorca, working in a large studio designed for him by the architect José Luis Sert. He never resumed his close contacts with the Surrealists, and it became increasingly evident that Miró's goal had never really been the same as theirs. His own evolution, like Arp's, took him ever closer to nature, but in the sense of the Chinese painter who said "I don't imitate nature; I work like her." Miró's unique forms and signs—birds, stars, suns, trees, women, "personages," animals—became progressively simplified and refined over the years, as they approached the "absolute of nature," and finally even these signs vanished, to be replaced by the free play of Miró's ravishing colors in luminous space.

His reputation has grown swiftly since 1941, the date of the important Miró retrospective in New York put on by The Museum of Modern Art, and nowhere has his influence been greater than in the United States. The lyrical abstractionists of the New York School, led by Jackson Pollock and Willem de Kooning, freely acknowledged their debt to Miró. Their exploitation of chance and the accidental effects of dripping paint were anticipated by Miró's experiments in the 1920s—although it should be noted here that, unlike Pollock, Miró exploited the possibilities of accident and chance only as a first stage in his composition: "The first stage is free, unconscious," he once said, "but after that the picture is controlled throughout, in keeping with that desire for disciplined work I have felt from the beginning." In the whole field of modern art, Miró today is considered second only to Matisse as a colorist, and the American critic Clement Greenberg has observed that his style "is so incorporated by now in [our contemporary world's] visual sensibility that no one who paints ambitiously can afford to be unaware of it."

Feeling the need to expand his creative field, Miró, like Picasso, also turned to sculpture and to the ceramic art. In collaboration with the master ceramist José Llorens Artigas (a classmate of Miró's at the Galí Academy in Barcelona), he created more than 200 ceramic works, including the ceramic "walls" at Harvard University and at the UNESCO Headquarters in Paris, for which latter he was awarded the Guggenheim Prize in 1959. This was also the year of his second major retrospective at The Museum of Modern Art.

Today, as he constantly explores new possibilities, experimenting with texture and proving, for example, that he can paint beautifully on cardboard or masonite, the only predictable certainty is that Miró's art will never cease to grow and evolve according to its own laws. "What really counts is to strip the soul naked," Miró said in 1936. "Painting or poetry is made as one makes love—a total embrace, prudence thrown to the winds, nothing held back." That is the way Joan Miró paints.

In 1947 Miró was commissioned to design a mural for the restaurant of the Terrace Plaza Hotel in Cincinnati. He painted the large canvas—9 by 32 feet—alone in New York in eight months, having studied the site: a circular room with wide windows. The colorful, gaily drawn work, painted in red, yellow, green and black on a soft blue ground, was subsequently moved to the Cincinnati Art Museum.

135

Two Giants
of Surrealism

Beyond the fact that they were both born in the
Spanish province of Catalonia, Salvador Dali and Joan
Miró had little in common—yet they were among the
most original and influential of all the Surrealists.

Miró's life, according to his biographer Jacques Dupin,
was always "completely lacking in adventure." Small, quiet,
unassuming, Miró found the sole outlet for his energies
in his exuberant, fanciful art, "I feel a great sympathy
for children," he once said, "a smile, a burst of laughter,
a shout, a word no one can understand, which only the child
understands...." His paintings, with their cryptic
ideograms and luminous, almost incandescent, colors,
are deliberately childlike—but far from unsophisticated.
"Joan Miró's genius," wrote critic James Johnson
Sweeney, "is the gift of growing young as he grows old."

Dali's life, on the other hand, has been a continual
series of violent explosions. A complete extrovert, he
once showed up at a news conference with green goggles
over his eyes and a boiled lobster on his head. He was nearly
murdered by members of Barcelona art society when
he attacked their recently deceased founder as "that
immense hairy putrefaction." His autobiography is
studded with exclamations like "How great he is! Look how
great Salvador Dali is!" Though his exhibitionism
eventually alienated most of the serious art world, his
early "hand-painted dream photographs" came close to
bearing out his own evaluation of himself as a genius.

Cats, easels, chairs, a torrent of water and Salvador Dali all appear to defy gravity as the artist interprets for the photographer the spirit of his *Leda Atomica*, partly obscured at right, in which his wife, Gala, is shown suspended in midair.

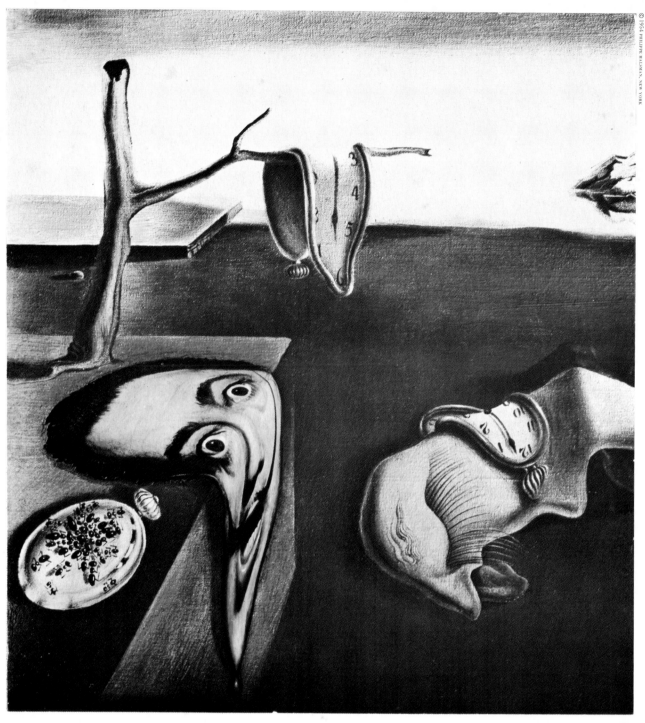

Philippe Halsman: altered photograph of Salvador Dali's *Persistence of Memory*, 1954

One of the best-known of all Surrealist works is Dali's *Persistence of Memory*; the sagging watches are so closely identified with him that he is almost interchangeable with them, as in the sleight-of-face portrait above. Dali's explanation of the painting explains little, in the finest Surrealist tradition: "Nothing is gayer than the persistence of memory. Soft watches . . . are masochistic because they are so eternal. Like filets of sole, they are destined to be swallowed by the sharks of mechanical time. Like Camembert cheese, they are also mystical, St. Augustine having said, in the Psalms of the Bible, that cheese can be assimilated to the body of Christ."

Even eerier images appear in *Accommodations of Desire*; its multiple lion heads, in various stages of incompletion, are intended "to turn the desire inside out like a stocking in order to expose to the sun the smallest wrinkles of the terrifying pleasures which were inside." To a viewer who requested a more intelligible explanation of his symbols, Dali replied, "It is enough to do the painting, much less try to understand it."

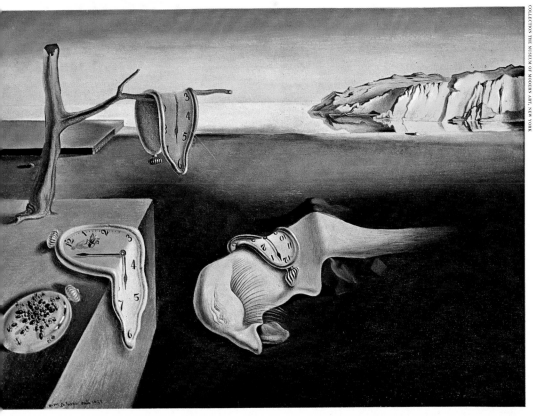

Salvador Dali: *The Persistence of Memory*, 1931

Salvador Dali: *Accommodations of Desire*, 1929

Salvador Dali: *Soft Construction with Boiled Beans: Premonition of Civil War*, 193(

The political climate in Spain before the Civil War affected many artists, and Dali was no exception. Early in 1936 he anticipated the tragedy in *Soft Construction with Boiled Beans: Premonition of Civil War*. "I showed a vast human body breaking out into monstrous excrescences of arms and legs tearing at one another in a delirium of autostrangulation," he wrote. As for the boiled beans, "one could not imagine swallowing all that unconscious meat without the presence . . . of some mealy and melancholy vegetable."

In a lighter vein is *The Invisible Man*. As the title implies, the man *is* invisible—until the viewer realizes that Dali has created a multiple image by using visual puns—clouds, for instance, form the hair on the man's head. The painting expresses Dali's feeling that people often experience a kind of negative hallucination—like the misplaced car keys that turn up in plain view after a long search. He claims an even more peculiar experience: he was once carrying an eight-foot-long loaf of bread when he tripped, dropped it—and never saw it again.

Salvador Dali: *The Invisible Man*, 1929-1933

Jan Vermeer (1632-1675): *The Lacemaker*

Dali's extraordinarily polished technique has often been compared with that of Jan Vermeer, the 17th Century Dutch painter who is often cited for his masterful use of light to define form. Dali cheerfully acknowledges his debt to Vermeer but points out that "instead of being content to paint the objects I see, I paint the visions that come into my head as a result of them." A typical example of Dali's visions is his interpretation of Vermeer's *Lacemaker*. He worked on the painting in two different locations: in front of *The Lacemaker* in the Louvre—and at the rhinoceros cage of a zoo. "I had to make [it] explode in the form

Salvador Dali: *Paranoiac-Critical Study of Vermeer's Lace-Maker*, 1955

of rhinoceros horns," he explained. "These horns [are] the ones in the animal kingdom constructed in accordance with [the] perfect logarithmic spiral . . . that guided Vermeer's hand in painting *The Lacemaker*."

Joan Miró, too, found inspiration in the Dutch masters. Their intimate realism revived in him a taste for familiar objects—but on his own terms. In *Dutch Interior II* he translated the realistic setting of a work by Jan Steen into a world of sheer fantasy. It is by no means a spoof of the old master; on the contrary, Miró admired and respected Steen almost to the point of reverence.

Jan Steen(1626-1679): *The Cat's Dancing Lesson*

Joan Miró: *Dutch Interior II*, 1928

Joan Miró: *The Farm*, 1921-1922

One of Miró's last realistic paintings was *The Farm*:
he was about to leave home for Paris, and according to his
biographer Jacques Dupin he "was trying to capture in
one last embrace all the rich reality of the place which
remains his most precious possession." The painting was
bought by Ernest Hemingway, who said, "I would not
trade it for any picture in the world."

Two years later, in *Catalan Landscape (The Hunter)*,
recognizable shapes have been replaced with symbols in
Miró's work. Near the left stands the hunter, with his
mustache, straggly beard and pipe; in one hand he holds a
leashed dog, in the other a shotgun. The "SARD" may be
the beginning of "Sardine"—Miró, often guided by free
association, had just painted a picture of a fish.

The ladder in *Dog Barking at the Moon* is usually
interpreted as a link between the physical world and the
realm of the intellect. *Person in the Presence of Nature*,
reflects Miró's agony over the impending war in Spain.

144

Joan Miró: *Catalan Landscape (The Hunter)*, 1923-1924

Joan Miró: *Dog Barking at the Moon*, 1926

145

Joan Miró: *Person in the Presence of Nature*, 1935

Joan Miró: *Bird*, 1945

I n 1933 Miró found himself driven by a
compulsion to distill his art down to a most basic
level. In a series of 18 extraordinary canvases, each
of which was titled *Painting*, Miró deliberately
purged his art of all extraneous elements,
recasting and refining every line and every shape
until it became, as a biographer put it, "the naked
archetype from which form springs."

To realize his goal, Miró felt that he had to
reject, or at least bypass, his own imagination.
To do this, he pieced together collages made of
photographs of screw drivers, carburetors and
other mundane devices. Then, on a bare canvas,
he began to paint, scrupulously adhering to the
overall design of the collage—but permitting the
individual elements to assume whatever form they
seemed to demand. When he had finished, the
banal objects were transformed into works of art
which critics consider some of the finest Miró
ever produced. And what he had done on canvas,
he did with equal success in sculpture.

Can these works, in which little or nothing is
recognizable, be called abstractions? Not if Miró
has anything to say about it. "Every shape, every
color . . . is derived from a piece of reality," he
said. "Everything in my pictures exists. . . .
There is nothing abstract in my pictures."

146

Joan Miró: *Painting*, June 10, 1933

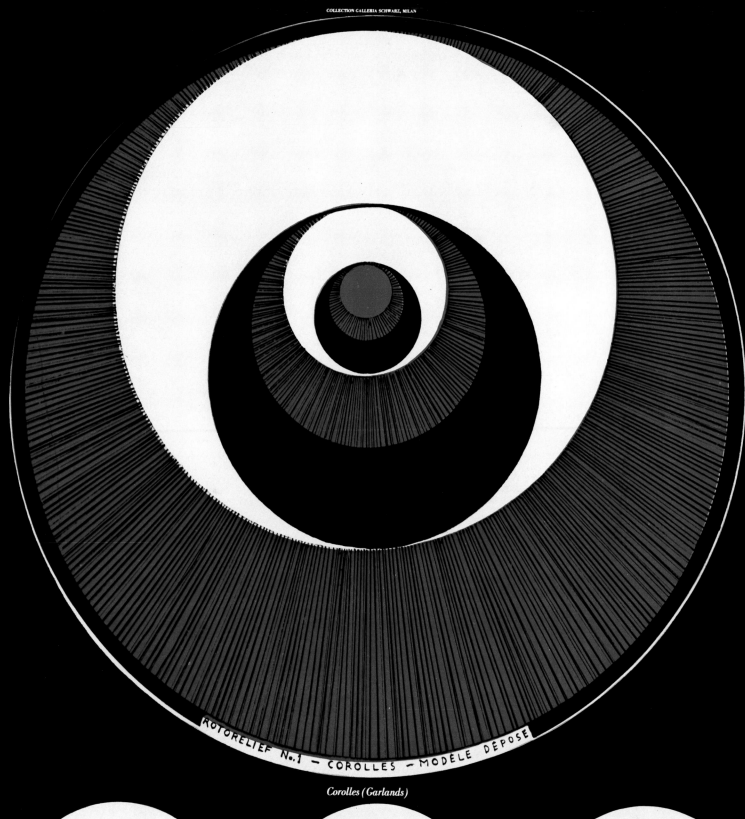

Corolles (Garlands)

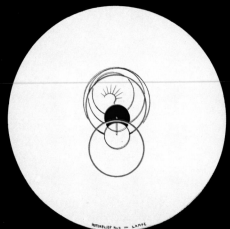

Lampe (Light Bulb)

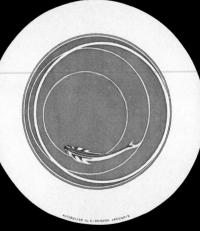

Poisson Japonais (Japanese Fish)

Montgolfière (Fire-balloon)

VII

A New Art
in America

*Painting is not for me either decorative amusement, or the plastic invention
of felt reality; it must be every time: invention, discovery, revelation.*

—MAX ERNST

The Surrealist painters in Paris had exhibited together since 1925, first
at the Galerie Pierre and from 1926 on at their own Galerie Surréaliste
on the Rue Jacques Callot. For many years their work was received with
open hostility by the general public and the critics. During the 1930s,
nevertheless, Surrealist painting virtually conquered the international
art world.

As an alternative to the highly intellectual esthetics of Cubism and
abstract art, Surrealism had from the outset exerted a powerful attraction for young artists in many countries. New recruits arrived each
year in Paris. Victor Brauner, a Romanian, came from Bucharest in
1930, and began to paint—in the manner of de Chirico—strange half-
human figures that might have been derived from the novels of Franz
Kafka. Oscar Dominguez from Tenerife in the Canary Islands made
his mark the following year with precisely painted "magic image" pictures reminiscent of Dali's. Wolfgang Paalen, an Austrian living in
Paris, was suddenly converted in 1935 from abstract art to Surrealism,
to which he contributed the technique of *fumage*, or interpreting the
smudge marks left by a candle flame applied to the surface of the canvas. Other young artists such as Belgium's Paul Delvaux became Surrealists without leaving home.

From 1935 on, the fame of the movement was also spread by a number of Surrealist exhibitions outside France—in Copenhagen, Prague,
Tenerife, Tokyo, Santiago de Chile and other cities. The two most
important of these large group shows were held in 1936—one in London and the other in New York. The International Surrealist Exhibition in London, which took place in June at the New Burlington
Galleries, showed the work of 60 artists from 14 countries, and it was
accompanied by an important monograph on Surrealism written by the
critic Herbert Read. The New York show opened in December at The
Museum of Modern Art, whose energetic and extremely influential director, Alfred H. Barr Jr., borrowed a leaf from P. T. Barnum in billing
it, quite justifiably, as "the biggest Surrealist show on earth." All in
all, the Museum brought together 700 items by nearly a hundred artists.

Experimenting with optical
phenomena, Duchamp designed
these patterned discs to be
"played" on a phonograph
turntable where, viewed with one
eye closed, they give amazing
illusions of depth. True to his
intention not to create "art,"
Duchamp "manufactured" 500
sets of the discs.

Rotoreliefs, 1935
(Top, actual size)

In his installation of these works and in the 250-page exhibition catalogue, Barr provided the kind of historical perspective and lucid, illuminating scholarship that the Museum has continued ever since to provide for modern art movements. Though sometimes called a taste-maker, Barr could more accurately be considered an educator who has served the cause of modern art as brilliantly as Bernard Berenson did the Renaissance. His 1936 show went a long way toward establishing Surrealism as a recognized force in art history, and it also pointed out clearly the essential difference between Surrealism, with its literary and extravisual associations, and the purely plastic, formal —or as Duchamp would say, "retinal"—painting that constitutes the other mainstream in art. "It should . . . be stated that Surrealism as an art movement is a serious affair and that for many it is more than an art movement," Barr said in his preface, and added: "It is a philosophy, a way of life, a cause to which some of the most brilliant painters and poets of our age are giving themselves with consuming devotion." This was the movement's great strength, at least in the beginning. As the Surrealist artists gained recognition and a measure of worldly success, they inevitably tended to lose interest in Surrealist goals, the foremost of which had been to "change life."

The activity that remained the purest in this sense was undoubtedly the creation of Surrealist *objects.* A number of these curious items were exhibited in the 1936 Museum of Modern Art show, including the famous *Fur-covered cup, plate and spoon (page 152)*—the work of a striking, black-haired, highly unfettered Swiss girl named Meret Oppenheim, who joined the movement in the mid-'30s. In his book *The History of Surrealist Painting,* Marcel Jean described such Surrealist objects as "points of reference of a universe which is separate from everyday life but still connected to it by the taut, solid threads of desire." In one sense these objects were concrete manifestations of the weirdly conceived but realistically drawn enigmas in the paintings of de Chirico, Dali, Magritte and other "magic image" Surrealists; they were also deliberate dislocations of reality, in the spirit of Lautréamont's image of "the chance meeting upon a dissecting table of a sewing machine and an umbrella." Marcel Duchamp's readymades and Man Ray's early object-ideas were certainly an important influence in this respect—particularly Duchamp's 1914 *Bottle Rack.* But the first truly Surrealist object was created in 1930 by a newcomer to Surrealist ranks, the Swiss sculptor Alberto Giacometti.

The son of a fairly well-known Post-Impressionist painter, Giacometti received a traditional art education at the Ecole des Arts-et-Métiers in Geneva. He spent nearly two years studying in Italy, and in 1922 went to Paris, where he worked in the studio of the famous sculptor Antoine Bourdelle, Rodin's spiritual heir. He met the Surrealists in 1930. Soon afterward, he began making sketches for "mute and mobile objects," several of which were published in *Le Surréalisme au Service de la Révolution.* The first took concrete shape the following year. It consisted of a metal framework from which hung a wooden ball on a string, suspended so that it barely grazed a crescent-shaped wedge on

Decalcomania, a Surrealist technique invented by Oscar Dominguez, consisted in smearing gouache on a glossy surface and then pressing paper onto the paint while moving it, thereby creating a highly accidental design. Dominguez called such exploratory works "Decalcomanias with no preconceived object."

the platform beneath. *Suspended Ball* was followed during the next four years by a number of equally enigmatic and vaguely disturbing objects that were greatly admired by the Surrealists. "For some years now," Giacometti wrote in 1934, "I have made only sculptures which offered themselves already completed to my imagination; I have limited myself to reproducing them in space without changing anything."

The best-known and most haunting of these was the construction now in The Museum of Modern Art, which Giacometti called *The Palace at 4 A.M. (page 153)*. As the artist said: "This object took shape little by little in the late summer of 1932; it revealed itself to me slowly, the various parts taking their exact form and their precise place within the whole. By autumn it had attained such reality that its actual execution in space took no more than one day."

Giacometti made his last object-sculpture in 1934; it is a figure of a woman clasping between her hands some invisible shape and it is called *The Invisible Object*. Later he renounced all his Surrealist work as "worthless, fit for the junk heap," and embarked on an entirely different course. His sole objective, he said, was to "put into place" a human head. The image that obsessed him from then on—which he has expressed in hundreds of sculptures showing an emaciated, eroded, stick-thin human figure—gradually came to be recognized as a uniquely powerful symbol of the loneliness and alienation of man in this century.

Most of the objects produced by the other Surrealists during the 1930s lacked the sculptural solidity and simplicity of Giacometti's work. Dali, for example, went in for highly elaborate concoctions having an erotic significance of some kind; he was particularly proud of his *Aphrodisiac Jacket*, a man's dinner jacket garnished with 40 cordial glasses filled with green liquid, at the bottom of each of which rested a dead fly. Breton himself made "object-poems"—collages of objects and poetic phrases. Picasso at this time made a number of sculptures from bits of scrap iron, rags, string and other *"objets trouvés"*—an activity that he would return to at intervals throughout his career, and which would produce such stunning metamorphoses as *Bull's Head*, made from a castoff bicycle seat and handlebars (1943), and *Baboon and Young*, whose head is a child's model automobile (1951). Miró created some highly intriguing objects, the most famous being his 1936 *Objet Poétique (page 132)*, a stuffed parrot atop a block of wood in whose hollowed-out center dangles a woman's leg. Man Ray's 1923 *Object to Be Destroyed (page 94)* was a metronome with a cut-out photograph of a human eye clipped to its pendulum. Most of these were shown in the first Exhibition of Surrealist Objects, in Paris in 1936, along with a great number of natural objects—stones, shells, fossils, et cetera, *objets trouvés*, primitive fetishes and "perturbed objects"—items that had suffered the effects of some natural catastrophe, such as a partially melted wineglass found in the ruins of a house on the island of Martinique after the 1902 eruption of Mont Pelée. Also included were three Duchamp readymades—*Bottle Rack*, *Why Not Sneeze?* and *Brawl at Austerlitz*.

Duchamp had become by this time a shadowy, almost legendary presence. Few of the Surrealists ever saw him, although he had been living

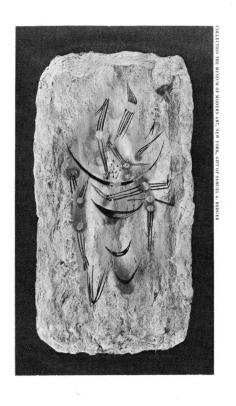

Fumage was the process invented by Wolfgang Paalen, who developed compositions from the sooty trail left by candle smoke. Like most Surrealists who used such "automatic" methods, in which the initial stimulus came from the subconscious, Paalen consciously added imagery to complete the work.

more or less regularly in Paris since 1923. When he was not playing in a chess tournament somewhere, he spent much of his time with Mary Reynolds, an attractive American woman whose husband had been killed in the First World War, and whose independent income enabled her to live comfortably in Paris and to maintain a house in Villefranche. This long and happy association was interrupted briefly in 1927, when Duchamp astonished everyone who knew him by marrying the daughter of a well-known French automobile manufacturer. Since Duchamp never discussed his private life, very little is known about this seemingly inexplicable union. Some considered it a sort of Dadaistic joke (albeit a cruel one) carried out to humor Duchamp's old friend Picabia. Man Ray has written that Duchamp spent most of the one week they lived together studying chess problems, and that one night, in retaliation, his bride got up and glued the chess pieces to the board. They were divorced four months later. Duchamp went back to his little studio on the Rue Larrey—which has entered art history by means of a Duchamp-designed, paradoxical door that served alternately to close either the bathroom or the main entrance, and could thus be both open and shut at the same time. He also resumed his pleasant relationship with Mary Reynolds, which lasted until her death in 1950 and which was looked upon by their mutual friends as better than most marriages.

Meret Oppenheim's fur-lined teacup stole the show at the 1936 Surrealist exhibition in New York, just as Duchamp's *Nude* had been the highlight of the Armory Show. An ordinary cup, saucer and spoon covered with brown rabbit fur, the "object" is a perfect expression of the Surrealist idea of dislocated reality.

In 1934, Duchamp published his "notes" for the *Large Glass*, in a limited edition of 300 copies. They were reproduced just as he had written them—on the same size scraps of paper, using the same color inks, duplicating even the underlinings and deletions and corrections —and instead of binding them together he had each set placed loosely in a cardboard box, in no particular order, so as to avoid the danger of overly logical interpretations. This *Green Box* of 1934 was thus the first public revelation of a whole new aspect of Duchamp's major work —the original ideas for what he had once called a "wedding of mental and visual relations" in which "the ideas . . . are more important than the actual visual realization."

Difficult as it was to decipher these rough jottings, most of which were couched in Duchamp's playful and highly complex intellectual shorthand, André Breton made a brilliant attempt at it. His beautiful and poetic essay "Lighthouse of the Bride," which appeared in the December 1934 issue of *Minotaure*, was the first important monograph on Duchamp, and it laid the basis for Duchamp's future reputation. Stressing the perfect balance of rational and nonrational concepts in the *Large Glass*, Breton concluded that Duchamp's unfinished masterpiece ranked among the most significant works of the 20th Century, a magical lighthouse whose purpose was "to guide future ships on a civilization which is ending."

Duchamp's continuing interest in motion and optics led him in 1935 to produce a set of six round cardboard disks that he called *Rotoreliefs (page 148)*. At rest, the disks appeared to be stamped with an abstract design, but when they were placed on a phonograph turntable and revolved, each design gave the illusion of a three-dimensional object— champagne glass, boiled egg in a cup, et cetera. Hoping perhaps to fulfill

Apollinaire's prediction that he was destined "to reconcile art and the people," Duchamp rented a booth at the annual gadget and invention show in Paris, the Concours Lépine, and exhibited his *Rotoreliefs*. The people were not to be reconciled. They stared at the disks with apparent curiosity before passing on to the garbage compressing device on the right or the vegetable chopper on the left, but nobody bought one.

It is possible that Duchamp's re-acquaintance with his own masterpiece in 1936—he spent two months that spring repairing the shattered *Large Glass* in a garage behind Katherine Dreier's house in Connecticut —may have stirred his artistic conscience for the first time in many years. The inclusion of 11 of his works in the big "Fantastic Art, Dada, Surrealism" show at the Museum of Modern Art later that year conceivably had its effect also. In any case, he began about this time to take a somewhat more active part in the art world, and the natural beneficiaries of his interest were the Surrealists. At Breton's invitation, Duchamp collaborated on the installation of the 1938 International Exhibition of Surrealism in Paris, a sensational event that provided, for the first time, a totally Surrealist setting for Surrealist art.

Although the 1938 show was a ringing success, Surrealism by this time had lost its inner cohesion. Most of the founding members had quarreled with Breton at one time or another, and either had left or had been expelled from the movement. The artists no longer saw each other regularly. Arp lived outside Paris in the suburb of Meudon, striving to create sculpture that would "find its humble, anonymous place in the woods, the mountains, in nature." His "Concretions" and other works in stone and wood were rooted in nature's forms and therefore no more abstract than Miró's "signs" for men, birds, stars; and, like Miró, as he penetrated ever deeper into the absolute of nature, Arp was moving away from Surrealist goals. Dali and Masson, although they contributed to the 1938 exhibition, were on bad terms with Breton. Max Ernst had gone to the South of France with Leonora Carrington, a beautiful and high-strung English girl from a well-to-do family, a self-taught artist who became a Surrealist upon meeting Ernst. Infuriated by Breton's order to "sabotage in every possible way the poetry of Paul Eluard" (who had left Surrealism to join the Communist Party), Ernst had decided in 1938 to sever his contacts with the movement.

Surrealism—or at any rate Surrealist painting—might simply have petered out at this point, if the War had not intervened and brought about a fresh coalition of the leading spirits in the stimulating atmosphere of New York. Some arrived early and without difficulty: Dali and Gala were in residence at the Hotel St. Regis by August 1940; Yves Tanguy, declared medically unfit for service in France, made the crossing in 1939 and later settled in Woodbury, Connecticut, with his American wife, the painter Kay Sage. Others were less fortunate. Max Ernst, who had retained his German citizenship, was interned by the French in 1939. Released, then interned again at the start of the German offensive in 1940, he escaped from a detention camp near Nîmes, was recaptured, then escaped again and found temporary refuge in Marseilles with the Emergency Rescue Committee, a private American organiza-

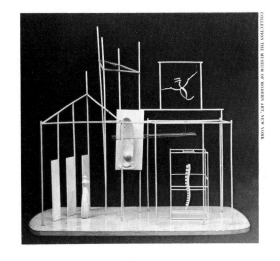

The Palace at 4 A.M., Alberto Giacometti's fragile little mansion constructed from thin wooden rods was something of an enigma to its creator. Of his sculpture's strange juxtaposition of elements Giacometti said, "I don't know why it's inhabited by a backbone in a cage. . . . On the other side is placed the statue of a woman, in which I discover my mother as she impressed my earliest memories. . . . I can say nothing of the object on a board which is red; I identify with it."

153

tion dedicated to helping bring European artists and scientists to the United States. Here he met and was partially reconciled with Breton. He also met Peggy Guggenheim, the American heiress, who had recently acquired a magnificent collection of modern art in France and was trying to get it back to New York. Miss Guggenheim's passion for modern art was exceeded only by her passions for modern artists—Tanguy and Duchamp, among others—and she soon found herself "madly in love" with Ernst, as she put it later in her autobiography, and determined "to save him from Europe and get him to New York." They arrived in July 1941, and were married soon afterward. In 1942, Miss Guggenheim opened her Art of This Century Gallery on West 57th Street; for the next few years this was the headquarters of Surrealism.

By then, the Surrealist group in America included Breton, Ernst, Tanguy, Masson, Man Ray, Kurt Seligmann, Dali (shunned by all the others), and the Chilean Matta, a relative newcomer who was destined to play a catalytic role in the development of several American artists. Among the non-Surrealist European artists who had taken refuge in the United States were such great names as Marc Chagall, Fernand Léger, Piet Mondrian and Jacques Lipchitz. This sudden influx of European ideas and energies had an electrifying effect on the group of American artists just coming to maturity in New York.

American art in the early 1940s was still largely provincial. With few exceptions, the American painters had retreated from experimental modernism after the 1913 Armory Show in which they were so completely overshadowed by the more advanced Europeans. Thomas Hart Benton, Edward Hopper and other realists of the older generation had been content, during the intervening three decades, to depict various aspects of the American scene. This no longer appealed to the younger group in New York. They wanted to assimilate the advances made by the Europeans, whose work they knew mainly from magazines, but so far they had not progressed much beyond inferior imitations of Picasso and Miró. For several of these Americans—Jackson Pollock, Arshile Gorky, Willem de Kooning and Franz Kline—Surrealism now became the key.

They did not become Surrealists—far from it. Valuing instinct above intellect, the Americans admired the Surrealists' spontaneity but they considered Surrealist painting far too theoretical and "literary." What they did was to take over the techniques of automatism and apply them to new and decidedly nonliterary ends. Masson's automatic drawing and painting, Miró's thin washes of paint that ran and dripped, all the accidents and interventions of chance that the Surrealists welcomed were now adopted by the Americans as keys to a new form of romantic, vigorously subjective art, an art of raw sensation. In Pollock's case it was a technique of Max Ernst's that pointed the way to his own discoveries. Ernst had been experimenting with a trick that he called "oscillation," which consisted of tying a string to a tin can, punching a small hole in the bottom, filling the can with paint and then swinging it over a canvas stretched flat on the floor, so that the paint described a series of flowing, interlacing arcs on the surface. For Ernst this was merely a beginning, a means to "force inspiration." As he did with his "decalcomanias" (the gouache technique first used by Dominguez, which Ernst applied to oil painting), he always went on to *interpret* the shapes and lines produced, scraping away and adding and overpainting until he had achieved a work that was densely packed with complex visual imagery. What Pollock did in 1947 was to take Ernst's oscillation technique and use it as an end in itself, a means of pouring his own unconscious impulses out upon the canvas through the violent "act" of painting. The gesture became the subject. This was Pollock's great breakthrough into Action Painting, the first native American style to gain international renown.

Although Pollock, de Kooning, Clyfford Still, Mark Rothko, William Baziotes, David Hare and other young Americans met the Surrealists at Peggy Guggenheim's Art of This Century Gallery—which gave many of them their first one-man shows—for the most part they did not establish close relations with the older and more worldly Europeans. Breton spoke no English, for one thing, and he disliked Americans. Masson had settled near Tanguy in Connecticut. Ernst parted company with Peggy Guggenheim in 1942 and went to live, first on Long Island and then in Sedona, Arizona, with Dorothea Tanning, a young painter who had been included in a 1942 group show of 31 women at the Art of This Century ("I realized that I should only have had thirty women in the show," Miss Guggenheim lamented afterward). They were married in 1946, in a double ceremony with Man Ray and his new bride, in Los Angeles. The only Surrealist with whom the Americans did have much direct contact was Matta, whose Surrealism was decidedly unorthodox.

Roberto Sebastian Antonio Matta Echaurren, though born in Chile, was by temperament and heritage a Basque, with all the intense individualism and mercurial energy of that talented people. Both his parents were Basques—one French, the other Spanish. They moved to Chile where Matta was born in 1912, and where he received his early training as an architect. He came to Paris in the mid-'30s and worked for three years in the architectural studio of Le Corbusier. A reproduction of Duchamp's *Passage from the Virgin to the Bride* that appeared in the 1935 issue of *Minotaure* helped to turn his interest from architecture to painting, and this new direction was confirmed by his meeting with the Paris Surrealists, whom he officially joined in 1937. Matta's early paintings showed the influence of Tanguy and Miró, rather than the "magic images" of Dali and Magritte. The most abstract of all the Surrealists, he had set himself to paint the "moment of change" that he sensed in Duchamp's *Passage*, and this led him to explore the "inner space" of his own racing ideas. He was fascinated by the discoveries being made in the physical sciences and also by the attempts of contemporary philosophers, such as Heidegger, to cope with the rapidly changing context of modern life, and he felt that Surrealism, instead of limiting itself to exploring the unconscious, should take heed of all these new intellectual vibrations. In the molten, dissolving forms and blazing colors of Matta's paintings it is possible to decipher not only premonitions of war and devastation, but also, perhaps, the dawn of the atomic era.

Matta came to the United States in 1939 and settled with his wife in New York, where he soon met the whole group of young American art-

When photographs of Picasso's early Cubist constructions appeared in a magazine in 1913, all but one of the 40 subscribers canceled their subscriptions. His *Glass of Absinth (above)*, evolved from those works, disarmed some viewers with its interplay of reality and illusion—the glass and sugar cube are of painted bronze, the absinth spoon is a real one. However, by 1938, when Kurt Seligmann showed his "ultra furniture"—a footstool made from mannequin legs and a cushion *(below)*— gallery visitors were sophisticated enough to sit on it.

ists. He was approximately the same age as most of them (unlike Breton and Ernst, who were of a previous generation), and he spoke English fluently. "I found that they were absolutely ignorant of European ideas," Matta said recently. "They knew nothing about Rimbaud or Apollinaire, and they were just copying the outward forms of Picasso and Miró. I started to invite them in to my place once a week to talk about the ideas *behind* modern painting." Several of the Americans found themselves intensely stimulated by these discussions, which later evolved into the informal gatherings of the Eighth Street "Artists' Club" in which the New York School tested and formulated its ideas.

For Matta, as for many others in the Surrealist group, the most admirable and intelligent artist alive was Marcel Duchamp. Duchamp had come over later than the others, arriving only in 1942. He had spent the early years of the War in Paris, methodically packing his esthetic luggage in what he called the *Boîte-en-Valise (Box in a Suitcase)*. This was an ingeniously designed leather-covered box, about the size of an attaché case, whose sides opened out to form a sort of personal museum for small-scale reproductions of 68 of his works—paintings and readymades. Duchamp had 20 copies of each item made up by commercial printers and hardware supply houses, and turned over the intricate job of assembling each item in the individual boxes to a succession of needy friends. With the aid of a special pass procured for him by Gustave Candel, a cheese merchant and old friend of the Duchamp family, he was able to pose as a cheese buyer and thus to make several "business trips" through Occupied France to Marseilles, and on each trip he took out a batch of his reproductions. When he had them all safely in Marseilles he made his way to Lisbon and from there to New York, arriving in June 1942, with his *Boîtes-en-Valises* and very little else.

Of all the European artists in exile, only Duchamp seemed to feel completely at home. He did not miss the café life in Paris, having never been a café lover in the first place, and he had many American friends who enjoyed his company. He could be reached only by letter or telegraph: there was no telephone in his quarters, a small studio over a commercial building at 210 West 14th Street. William Copley, the American painter and collector, remembers seeing Duchamp's studio once and being impressed by its spartan décor. "It was a medium-sized room," Copley recalled. "There was a table with a chess board, one chair, and a kind of packing crate on the other side to sit on, and I guess a bed of some kind in the corner. There was a pile of tobacco ashes on the table where he used to clean his pipe. There were two nails in the wall, with a piece of string hanging down from one of them. And that was all." No one knew what he did there. When questioned, Duchamp would only say, with the greatest good humor, that he was a *"respirateur,"* a "breather," and that his financial arrangements were his own affair.

His influence nevertheless hovered sardonically over the New York scene. Soon after he arrived, Duchamp collaborated with Breton in assembling a large Surrealist exhibition for the benefit of French children and War prisoners in the old Villard mansion at 451 Madison Avenue. Duchamp transformed it for the occasion with a vast web of string. Certain dealers—Peggy Guggenheim and Sidney Janis in particular—used regularly to ask his advice about young painters. "Both Marcel and Mondrian liked things that were different from what they themselves had done," Janis said once. "They didn't have to protect their own point of view all the time, as so many painters feel obliged to do." In this respect, Duchamp's position was supremely ironic: considered the anti-artist of all time, the complete iconoclast who had once proposed, as a readymade, the use of a Rembrandt painting as an ironing board, he nevertheless worked quietly and generously to promote the careers of younger artists and to further the development of modern art.

When anyone asked a favor of him he seemed glad to comply. He designed the cover for the March 1943 issue of *VVV*, the Surrealist magazine that André Breton and Max Ernst had founded in New York as a successor to *Minotaure*. A reproduction of his rather disturbing collage entitled *George Washington (Allégorie de Genre)*, a portrait of the Founding Father done in bandage gauze, with stars and bloodstains, appeared in the next issue of *VVV*; it had been commissioned by *Vogue*, which rejected the result in some embarrassment. In 1945, his American reputation was enhanced by an exhibition of the three Duchamp brothers at the Yale University Art Gallery, and by a special issue of the art-literary magazine *View* that was devoted entirely to articles about Duchamp, his influence and his legend.

There was to be a 10-year hiatus, though, before Duchamp—still with no visible effort on his part—arrived at the legendary eminence he enjoys today. In New York the atmosphere was changing radically. Many of the European artists went home after the War. Peggy Guggenheim packed up her collection and moved to Venice. The Americans of the New York School were forging the new style of Action Painting that would soon sweep the international art world. Their art was highly "retinal" and aggressively antiliterary; understandably, the painters of this particular group were not interested in Duchamp—although Willem de Kooning, after Pollock's death in 1956 the acknowledged leader of the group, would remark at one point that Duchamp was "a one-man movement," but "a movement for each person and open for everybody."

For his own part, Duchamp elected to stay in New York and become an American. "I found in America a little better acceptance of my right to live," he said. "I have more friends, more real friends here than in France. It just happened—that's my luck. I find it better to belong here and to travel. Any place you stay in long enough becomes boring, I suppose, even Heaven. Especially Heaven. But there is more freedom here. In France, in Europe, the young men of any generation always act as grandsons of some great man; even the Cubists used to say they were all grandsons of Poussin, and so when they come to produce something of their own they find the tradition is indestructible. This does not exist in America. Americans don't give a damn about Shakespeare, do they? And that makes it a better terrain for new developments."

In the new developments of the next decade, however, the young American innovators would all come to regard themselves as grandsons of Marcel Duchamp.

Surrealism on Parade

Unlike other innovators in art, the Surrealists were not only interested in new departures in subject matter and style; they wanted to change the traditional form of the exhibits as well. What they aimed at was a "total artistic experience" in which art, environment and spectator would be completely intertwined. Thus, a Surrealist show was quite an occasion: walls were not simply hung with paintings; together with floors and ceilings they were decorated in fantastic ways, and bizarre furniture and strange lighting effects were often part of the spectacle. A fascinated public—responding with enthusiasm if not always with understanding—willingly contributed to the experience: so many people mobbed a Surrealist exhibition in Paris in 1938 that a cordon of police had to be called in to maintain order. A weary gendarme remarked afterward, "This show is the work of crazy people."

Crazy or not, the Surrealists achieved their aim. Some two decades later their ideas about integrating art, environment and observer found new expression in the "Happening," a form of theater introduced by Pop artists. Happenings owe much to Dada, in their simultaneous presentation of unrelated spectacles, and to Action Painting, in their emotional energy and vividly colored lights. But the Happening would probably never have happened without the precedent of Surrealism, a unique experiment in the age-old process of melding artist and viewer, described by Duchamp as "the two poles of creative art."

Visitors to the 1938 International Surrealist Exhibition in Paris were greeted by a line of mannequins, outfitted by various artists. Duchamp's model, wearing a man's jacket, hat and shoes, stands between a gauze- and flower-draped figure and André Masson's apparition with a bird-cage head.

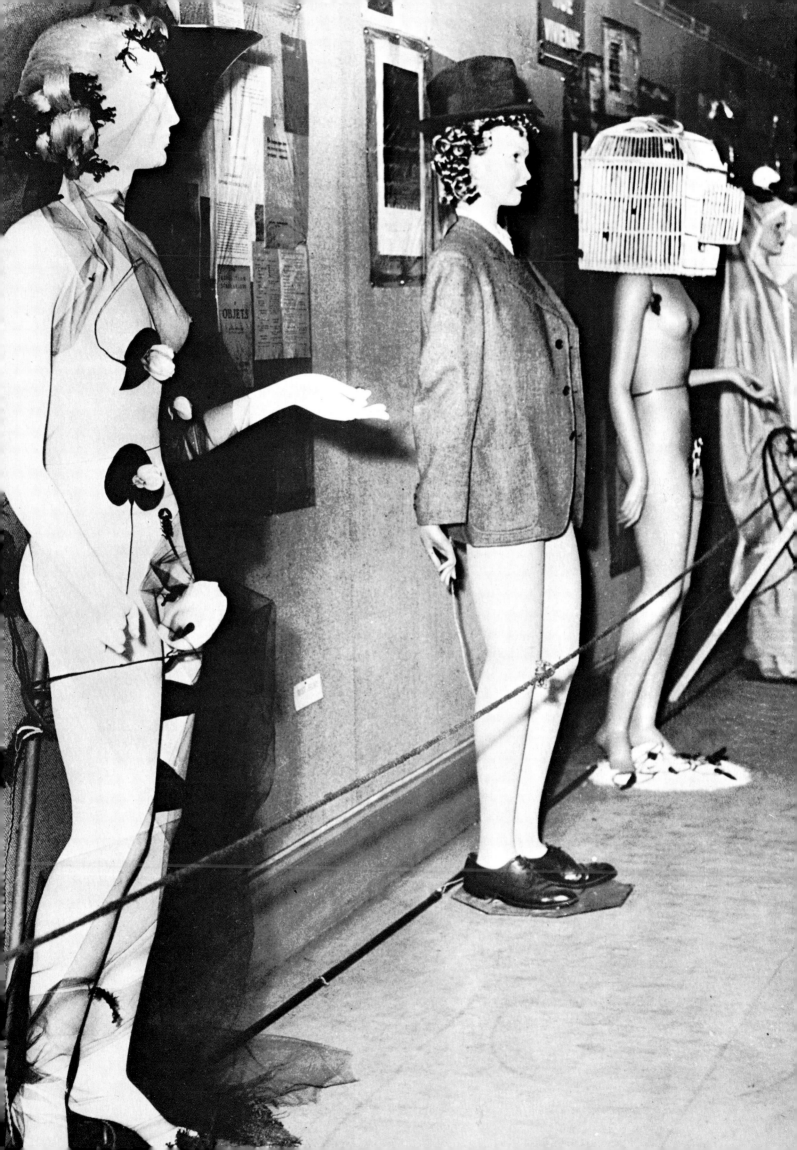

Flower-headed woman in Trafalgar Square, London, 1936

Humor was one of the ingredients that made many Surrealists' exhibitions such popular successes. The artists who put them together had fun, and so did the people who saw them. In 1936 Salvador Dali suggested that a London show be publicized by having a girl roam Trafalgar Square with her head enshrubbed in roses *(left)*. The public responded by flocking to the exhibit at the rate of 1,500 a day. "A shocking show," cried a *Daily Mail* headline, and most of the critics agreed. But such comments only boosted attendance.

Wildest of all the shows was the International Surrealist Exhibition in Paris in 1938. Marcel Duchamp,

Gramophone sculpture, International Surrealist Exhibition, Paris, 1938

though not a Surrealist, designed the show, transforming the central hall into a grotto carpeted with leaves and roofed with coal sacks. The room was in semidarkness, and visitors had to grope their way with flashlights (*right*). Weird objects were displayed, like a phonograph into whose horn a woman appeared to be crawling while a hand reached out from the other end (*below, left*). In another part of the exhibition stood Dali's *Rainy Taxi* (*below*), the shell of an old cab from whose ceiling fell an incessant downpour that doused the mannequin occupants: a driver with a shark's head and a frowzy blonde sharing the back seat with dozens of live snails.

Gallery-goers with flashlights, International Surrealist Exhibition, Paris, 1938

Salvador Dali: *Rainy Taxi*, International Surrealist Exhibition, Paris, 1938

International Surrealist Exhibition, New York, 1942

When Duchamp wove a maze of twine around the paintings at a Surrealist exhibition *(left)*, his purpose was the same as that of the creators of Happenings: to force the viewer to involve himself in his surroundings. "My aim is the perfection of events rather than any composition," said artist Claes Oldenburg, who created the event at right, in which his wife Pat was carried partly clad through a room to pick up a loaf of bread.

Happenings have been described as a form of theater that has a structure but no plot, words but no dialogue, actors but no characters and, above all, nothing logical or continuous. For example, at one Paris Happening a man massaged a masked girl with spaghetti atop a car *(bottom, right)*. And when a group of Surrealists posed for their picture *(below)*, they donned identical masks. Why? In "art" of this kind no help is given; the viewer must provide the answers for himself.

Claes Oldenburg: Scene from *Ray Gun Theater*, 1962

Jean-Jacques Lebel: Second Festival of Free Expression, Paris, 1965

Surrealists pose on an outing near Paris in 1958.

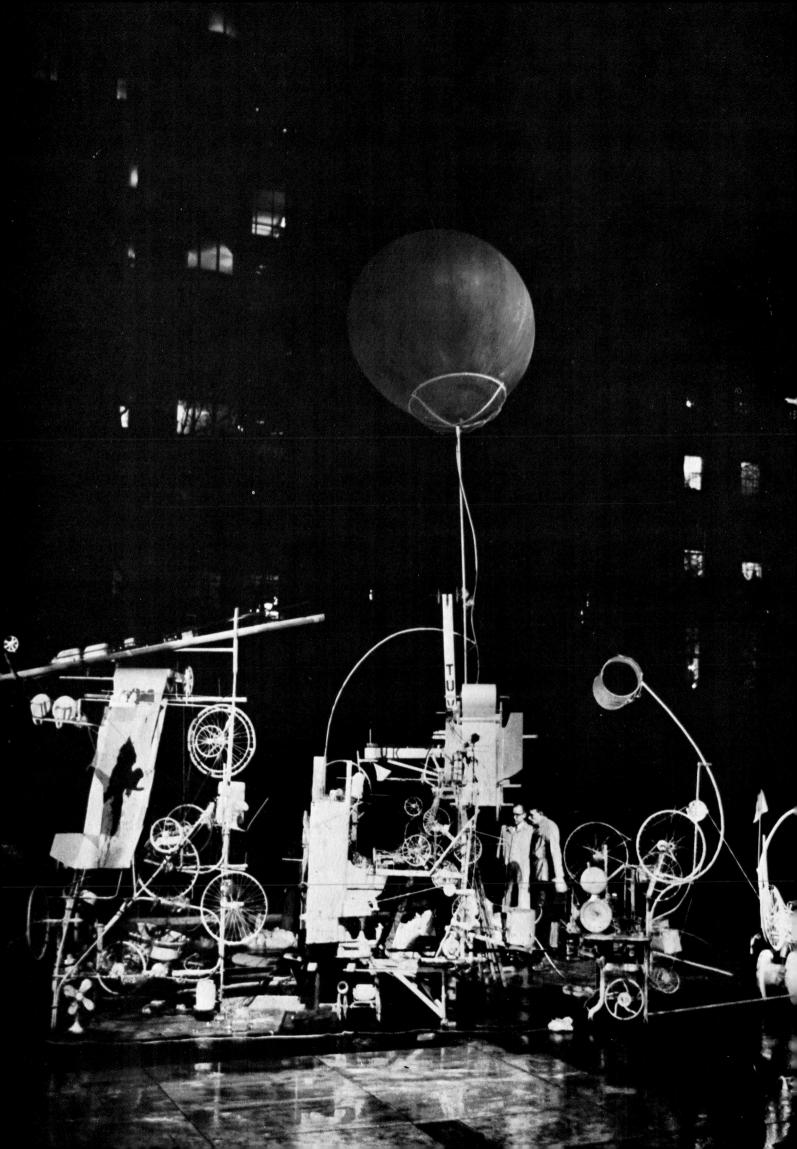

VIII

Idol of the Iconoclasts

I don't believe in art. I believe in artists. —MARCEL DUCHAMP

Jean Tinguely's motorized, explosive "junk sculpture" *Homage to New York* was designed to destroy itself in the garden of the Museum of Modern Art in New York in 1960. After it haltingly did so, Tinguely sat happily in the rubble signing fragments *(above)*.

Surrealism did not survive its period of exile. The European artists who returned home after 1945 no longer wished to adhere to a movement that placed limitations on their freedom. Ernst, Miró, Masson, Arp, Magritte, Man Ray and others of the older Surrealist warriors were beginning at last to receive the public recognition long denied them, and several even assumed positions among the "old masters" of modern art—a trend that was confirmed when the Venice Biennale gave its top prizes in 1954 to Max Ernst, Jean Arp and Joan Miró. For accepting this award from what Breton considered the corrupt art establishment, Ernst was formally expelled from the Surrealist movement.

Breton himself remained incorruptible. Resuming his role as absolute dictator of Surrealism in Paris, he continued to formulate policy, to enroll and expel members and to meet every day with his disciples at the officially designated Surrealist cafés. In the years following 1945 Breton staged several new Surrealist exhibitions such as the "Surrealism in 1947" show at the Galerie Maeght in Paris, for which Duchamp designed a special catalogue whose cover bore a life-sized foam-rubber replica of a female breast labeled *Prière de Toucher (Please Touch) (page 166)*. His total dedication to the cause commanded respect, but it had been clear for a long time before his death that Surrealism no longer existed outside his rigorous and intractable intelligence.

In New York, where Duchamp had become a permanent resident (and a U.S. citizen in 1955), the art world centered on the emerging New York School of "action" painters. Again Duchamp seemed to have become a peripheral figure. He played chess, but only for pleasure now. The dealer Roland Knoedler once asked Man Ray to approach Duchamp with the idea of his returning to painting—Knoedler was ready to offer him a $10,000-a-year contract if Duchamp would paint one picture a year. "When I broached the offer to Duchamp," Man Ray wrote, "he smiled and said that he had accomplished what he had set out to do and did not care to repeat himself." Duchamp seemed to prefer to turn out his suitcase museums, the *boîtes-en-valises*, which were being made in a new "edition" that would eventually number 300—it was the survival of his ideas that interested him.

Secretly, Duchamp was working on his last masterpiece *(opposite)* in his studio on New York's 14th Street. He had begun it in 1946 and continued until 1966. Although he never denied working on it, he implied that all he did was putter around, play chess and, as he put it, "breathe." This construction, *Given . . .* , is said to be one of his major works; it is linked with *The Large Glass* in concept and importance.

In the late 1950s, the esthetic seismographs began to detect new tremors emanating from New York. Ever since the first triumphs of Abstract Expressionism, conservative critics had been hopefully proclaiming its imminent demise and predicting a return to "humanist" themes. They were in for a shock. The new style, which emerged about 1960, was as anti-abstract as the critics could have wished, but its highly realistic subject matter came not from humanist themes but from the garish, dehumanized world of 20th Century advertising and so-called popular (i.e., mass) culture. The British critic Lawrence Alloway coined the term "Pop Art" to describe it, and the name stuck.

Pop Art confounded its many enemies—artists as well as critics—by the phenomenal speed with which it established itself worldwide. This was the first art movement to receive the benefit (if that is the word) of all-out publicity by 20th Century mass communications, and a vast amount of nonsense has been written about it. It has been linked with Surrealism, in that both were reactions against the "pure painting" of the dominant movement preceding them; but where Surrealism was essentially a romantic reaction against the formal, intellectual and, in a sense, classical ideal of Cubism, Pop was exactly the opposite, a decidedly unromantic reaction against the violent emotionalism of Action Painting. The new painters directed their attention outward, to the world around them, rather than inward upon their own reactions to it, and they kept their feelings to themselves. Their attitude shows certain affinities to Dadaism (the movement is often referred to, particularly in Europe, as "neo-Dada") but the resemblance is only superficial. The Dadaist methods were conceived as shock tactics in a total war against bourgeois culture; the Pop artists were not at war with anyone and they were not really trying to shock the viewer.

From the beginning, Pop Art was highly experimental. Its practitioners tested and used a wide variety of methods and materials, and they experimented constantly with new ideas. The younger generation was also utterly open-minded with regard to the perennially unresolved question, "What is art?", and it was therefore natural for its members to look with increasing reverence in the direction of the most open-minded artist of the century, who happened, conveniently enough, to be living on West 14th Street in New York, and whose rather belated emergence as one of the great figures in modern art coincided with their own artistic coming of age.

Several factors contributed to the renewal of interest in Duchamp during the 1950s. Walter Arensberg had died in 1954. Three months before, he and his wife (who predeceased her husband by a few months)

Each of the 999 de luxe copies of the catalogue cover Duchamp designed for the *Exposition Internationale du Surréalisme* had a foam rubber breast mounted on black velvet. Regular editions simply carried a photograph of the object. Like many other Duchamp parodies—magazine covers, posters, altered objects—this one has been elevated to the status of art and is often framed and hung.

had donated their collection to the Philadelphia Museum of Art, and in 1954 the Walter and Louise Arensberg Collection—one of the finest selections of modern masters ever assembled—went on permanent display in a special section of the Museum. With nearly all his major works thus gathered together in one place, the master of "anti-art" was once again revealed as a painter of remarkable gifts, and as an innovator second to none.

All this may have had some effect on Duchamp's private life, which was also starting to emerge from the shadows of solitude following Mary Reynolds's death in 1950. Shortly before his work went on display at the Philadelphia Museum in 1954, Duchamp abandoned what had seemed permanent bachelorhood and married for the second time. His new wife was Alexina Sattler, a charming and gracious woman known throughout the art world as "Teeny," and their life together in a pleasant apartment on West 10th Street, surrounded by modest bourgeois comforts, offered every evidence in the years that followed of being extremely happy. He was seen again from time to time at artistic gatherings, and he began to cooperate with those who sought to secure his reputation in art history. In 1958 a young professor of literature, Michel Sanouillet, brought out a volume with the suitably Duchampian anagrammatic title of *Marchand du Sel*, containing almost all of Duchamp's miscellaneous writings—including puns, anagrams, "verbal readymades," and the notes for the *Large Glass*. Duchamp gave every assistance to Sanouillet in preparing this collection, and the following year he collaborated closely with the French critic Robert Lebel on the design and illustrations for Lebel's book *Sur Marcel Duchamp*, an important survey of his career that was translated by George Heard Hamilton and published in an English edition in 1959. The Lebel book acquainted the new generation of New York artists with Duchamp's work and ideas at precisely the moment when these ideas assumed direct relevance to their own questions and preoccupations.

Duchamp's influence on the new young painters and sculptors was immense but characteristically indirect. The two most important artists of this generation—Robert Rauschenberg and Jasper Johns—had each charted his own individual course before becoming specifically aware of Duchamp's work. In the matter of painting style both men were much closer to the loose, sweeping brushwork and bold colors of Abstract Expressionism (which they had broken away from ideologically) than to the subdued colors and classic technique of Duchamp's mature paintings. It was in their experimental attitude and their iconoclasm that these two young painters felt close to Duchamp, whose example they found deeply reassuring.

R obert Rauschenberg, who grew up in the little Gulf Coast refinery town of Port Arthur, Texas, and who did not even know there was such a thing as art until he left home at 18 to join the Navy, was the first to embark on the new course. As an art student at Black Mountain College in North Carolina he learned from Josef Albers about the subtle effects that one color has upon another. Unwilling to put into practice what seemed to him purely arbitrary color choices and thus to make

A Spanish door—the only part of Duchamp's last masterpiece that may be photographed—guards *Given: 1. The Waterfall, 2. The Illuminating gas.* Only visitors to the Philadelphia Museum of Art can see what lies beyond the door: a construction consisting of a painted leather sculpture of a nude woman on a bed of real twigs and leaves, holding a gas lamp; behind that, in a photo-collage, a hilly, wooded landscape; and, at the far right, a mechanical light and plastic contraption simulating a waterfall, the only moving part of the tableau. One of Duchamp's last acts before his death was choosing the bricks surrounding the door.

color "serve" his private taste. he reacted by subsequently painting a series of all-white and all-black pictures which, together with several paintings consisting of dirt and one that incorporated growing grass, soon established him as the *enfant terrible* of the New York art scene.

Rauschenberg liked to think of his work as a form of "collaboration" with materials, rather than an imposition of his own order. He welcomed the element of chance, particularly in the acquisition of the various collage elements that began to appear in his paintings from 1953 on, and which tended to become progressively larger and more surprising. Electric light bulbs, parasols, doors, torn political posters, undershirts, Coke bottles, electric fans and scrap lumber were some of the elements that turned up in his early collage paintings, and he soon went far beyond those to include such "outrageous" artifacts as a stuffed eagle, a painted-on quilt and pillow, and an Angora goat with an automobile tire around its middle. The critics—and most of the Abstract Expressionists—recoiled in disgust from these curious "combines," as the artist called those of his works that combined both painting and sculpture. But Rauschenberg was not simply trying to shock; he was exploring the relationship between art and life, and attempting, as the Dadaists had done, to make something that was a piece of reality instead of an interpretation of it. "I think a picture is more like the real world when it's made out of the real world," was the way he put it.

The first public showing of Rauschenberg's 34 drawings of Dante's *Inferno*, at the Leo Castelli Gallery in 1960, persuaded even his detractors that Rauschenberg must be considered one of the foremost artists of the younger generation. His silk-screen paintings of the early and mid-1960s, adapted from a *frottage* technique he invented for the drawings, not only established Rauschenberg as one of the most successful and highly paid artists of his time but also secured his international reputation. In the late 1960s, Rauschenberg became a master printmaker, working at home and abroad with an enormous variety of materials and surfaces.

Jasper Johns, a largely self-taught painter from Allendale, South Carolina, came to New York in 1952 and had his first show at Leo Castelli's in 1958. Although Johns's work was in some ways as "difficult" as Rauschenberg's, it received the immediate approval of Alfred Barr Jr., who bought three Johns paintings for The Museum of Modern Art. From that moment Johns had a booming market and a reputation nearly equal to that of his slightly older contemporary.

It was Johns's implacable logical notion that since the surface of the canvas was flat, he would paint only flat images. He was not interested in producing an illusion or an interpretation of reality; like Rauschenberg, he wanted to make paintings that looked like what they were, and this led him to paint such familiar things as flags, targets, maps and numbers (one cannot paint an "image" of the number seven; one can only paint a seven), to all of which he was able to impart a striking intensity and power that made the viewer feel as though he were seeing them for the first time. Johns's style is far more elegant and "painterly" than Rauschenberg's, and his subject matter has tended to be more intellectual and less aggressive—and perhaps for this reason more easily acceptable. A great many of his paintings have really been "about" painting: large canvases in which brushes, paint cans and other studio fixtures appear as collage elements; works whose primary colors correspond (or fail to correspond) with stenciled words that refer to these colors; "self-portraits" made by smearing paint on his face and pressing it to the canvas.

The trail blazed by Rauschenberg and Johns was soon traveled by the younger group of Pop artists, with whom the two pioneers are often and mistakenly confused. Jim Dine and Claes Oldenburg exploited the total freedom that Rauschenberg had initiated in the field of collage, making paintings out of carpenters' tools and plumbing fixtures (Dine), commenting humorously on contemporary popular culture with eight-foot-wide hamburgers made of kapok (Oldenburg), and carrying the whole process a step further by staging "Happenings"—a form of theatrical performance in which the actors functioned as collage elements in a nonverbal, indeterminate series of visual situations.

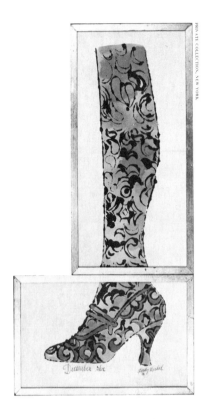

Andy Warhol's background as an illustrator of shoes and accessories for women's magazines is evident in his two-part painting *December Shoe (above)*. The famous *Campbell Soup Can (below)* is the embodiment of his dictum: "I paint things I always thought beautiful—things you use every day and never think about."

Roy Lichtenstein and James Rosenquist steered closer to Johns's course with paintings that had to do mainly with the act of painting. Lichtenstein became known for pictures derived from comic strips and advertisements, done in greatly enlarged scale and with a technique imitating the Benday dots of commercial engraving—a technique that referred back sardonically to the pointillist method of the Impressionists. Rosenquist, who had once worked as a professional sign painter specializing in huge display ads, juxtaposed enlarged details from the more garish advertising displays in the mass circulation magazines or on billboards. By far the most widely publicized member of the Pop establishment, the ex-advertising designer Andy Warhol, became a highly successful artist simply by pushing all these ideas still further. Warhol's silk-screened image of a Campbell soup can is perhaps the final apotheosis of the readymade.

As an international phenomenon that broke out in several countries at approximately the same time, Pop Art has assumed different forms according to its place of origin. The first truly Pop painting was probably a collage done by the British artist Richard Hamilton in 1956 *(page 170)*—it actually contained the word "POP" written on a giant lollypop in a living room full of advertising slogans and mass-production products. English Pop, like the Beatles, has tended to be witty, high-spirited, but basically well-behaved.

In Paris, where the movement first called itself *Le Nouveau Réalisme*, Pop has developed along more Dadaistic and intellectual lines. Yves Klein, the leading French "new Realist" until his death in 1962 at 34, once put on a highly provocative exhibition of nothing at all: the newly whitewashed Iris Clert Gallery in Paris was void of paintings or any other objects, and what the viewers witnessed—and in two cases even *bought* (by paying hard cash for two nonexistent canvases) —was simply the untrammeled presence of the artist.

Although the popular image of urban, 20th Century mass culture admits endless diversity, most of the young artists who are involved

in depicting it have certain attitudes in common. They do not believe in the religion of art. They are not out to create masterpieces that will alter the course of painting. They are skeptical, irreverent and extremely curious about the real nature and function of art in an existentially absurd era—the era of The Bomb. It is in this spirit that they all feel very close to Duchamp. Richard Hamilton spent two years arranging Duchamp's notes for the *Large Glass* in a "typographic facsimile," which appeared in book form in 1960, and he has made a painstakingly exact replica of the *Large Glass* itself, minus the cracks. English, French, Italian and even Japanese artists have painted works in homage to the "Grandada" of Pop. Rauschenberg acquired a signed replica of the *Bottle Rack* in 1959, and he has said that he finds "Duchamp's life and work a constant inspiration."

A great many contemporary artists working in other directions have felt much the same way. Duchamp's optical machines of the 1920s and 1930s anticipated the so-called "Op" artists who experiment with patterns that play on the idiosyncrasies of human perception. Few Op effects are more striking than Duchamp's cover design for a 1936 issue of *Cahiers d'Art:* two superimposed heart shapes, one blue and the other red, whose strongly contrasting colors cause the edges of the inner heart to appear to vibrate or flutter (the drawing is called *Coeurs Volants*, or *Fluttering Hearts*). Duchamp's experiments with motion—both simulated (as in *Nude Descending a Staircase*) and actual (as in his optical machines)—are important points of reference in the development of moving or kinetic art, which has emerged as one of the major recent preoccupations of artists in several countries.

D uchamp's best-known contribution to kinetic art was the term "mobile," which he coined in 1932 to identify Alexander Calder's gracefully balanced metal sculptures whose various parts reacted to moving currents of air. Various other methods of activating sculpture have been developed in recent years, and most of the kineticists are ardent admirers of Duchamp. When the Swiss motion sculptor Jean Tinguely came to New York for the first time in 1960 with the idea of building a large machine whose sole purpose would be to destroy itself in the garden of The Museum of Modern Art, he immediately sought and received Duchamp's blessing. Tinguely's *Homage to New York*, the huge machine that did in fact destroy itself in the Museum's garden, one memorable night in March 1960, impressed Duchamp as a gallant gesture and a last-ditch attempt to destroy art "before it's too late"— i.e., before the vital spirit drowned in the rising ocean of publicity, mass "appreciation," and immense but mediocre production.

Ironically enough, Duchamp's own production as an artist and even as an anti-artist received such public attention in the 1960s that the spirit behind it was in some danger of being forgotten. The big 1963 Duchamp exhibition at the Pasadena Art Museum in California—the first major retrospective show of his work ever presented anywhere—effectively canonized him as a patron saint of modern art. It also helped to create a bull market for Duchamp "replicas"—scale models of his more famous readymades and other objects, manufac-

Richard Hamilton's work *Just What Is It That Makes Today's Homes So Different, So Appealing?* is considered the first Pop painting. (In fact, the word "Pop" appears in it on the lollipop held by the muscle-man.) A collage of contemporary photographs, the work was first exhibited in London in 1956 in a show called "This Is Tomorrow." Hamilton, an English artist-teacher and admirer of Duchamp, also made a replica of the latter's nine-foot-high *Large Glass* and organized the Duchamp Retrospective Exhibition at London's Tate Gallery in 1966.

tured in limited editions and signed by Duchamp. An astute Milanese dealer named Arturo Schwarz put out eight sets of these replicas in 1965, each set containing 13 objects; he priced them at $25,000 per set and sold every one. Duchamp was amused by this total commercialization. He accepted his royalties without a qualm, and took pleasure in the fact that at an age well past 75, having done nothing but what he wanted to do all his life, he suddenly found himself able to travel first class and to spend his summers with Teeny on the Costa Brava. But he was not in the least deceived. Dealers, critics, collectors were just so many "lice on the back of the artists," he said in 1965, and their enthusiasms had nothing to do with anything outside the current frenetic art market.

"Society takes what it wants," Duchamp once said. "The artist himself doesn't count, because there is no actual existence for the work of art. The work of art is always based on the two poles of the onlooker and the maker, and the spark that comes from that bipolar action gives birth to something—like electricity. But the onlooker has the last word, and it is always posterity that makes the masterpiece. The artist should not concern himself with this, because it has nothing to do with him."

Having followed him thus far, can we sum up finally what it is that Duchamp represents? The wide range of his influence proves that, like Picasso, he cannot be pinned down to any particular style or single view of art's function. Duchamp remained the complete iconoclast. Nothing was sacred to him, certainly not the "habit-forming drug" called art. There is, however, an affirmative power behind his iconoclasm. Icons are to be worshiped, usually behind closed doors. By knocking over the esthetic icons wherever he found them, including the icons of his own cult, Duchamp performed the useful service of keeping all the doors open in the house of art. With humor and skepticism, he served as a living proof against the tendency of romantic artists to take themselves too seriously and the temptation of dogmatic theorists to turn new discoveries into academic formulas.

Despite the cynicism and mediocrity that characterize so much of what passes for art today, the doors have remained open, and anything, even great painting, remains possible. Although the powerful forces of the modern art market, of publicity and mass communications all conspire to distract him, the great artist can still go underground, as Duchamp often suggested. By refusing to deal with the money-society on its own terms he can preserve his freedom, without which no new contribution is ever made.

Looking behind Duchamp's iconoclasm, behind the broken glass of his major work, young artists have seen in him the continuing possibility of freedom in the pursuit of their ideas. Nothing is ever really settled in art. The goals are never defined once and for all, and in each generation a young artist must choose his own course and decide for himself about the nature of art and reality—or decide not to decide. No artist ever maintained his freedom more successfully than Duchamp, and in the long run this may come to be considered his most enduring work of art.

COURTESY ALVIN LANE AND HENRY KLEIN, NEW YORK

The delightful, moving sculptures of Alexander Calder were given the name "mobiles" by Duchamp in the 1930s. Calder's *Verticale Hors de l'Horizontale* (*above*) typifies the brightly painted, free-form shapes which, suspended from nearly invisible wires, sway, twist and spin at the lightest breath of air. Unlike conventional abstract sculpture, mobiles change shape constantly and redefine the space around them in infinite ways.

The Heirs of Duchamp

In the years since World War II a new generation of artists has appeared. Many were unborn when Duchamp abandoned painting, but most are indebted to him. Although he might have scoffed at the idea, his position as a patron saint of modern art is assured.

The first and most influential style of the new art was Abstract Expressionism. As practiced by such artists as Jackson Pollock, Arshile Gorky and Franz Kline, it evolved at least partly from Surrealist principles, especially in the use of "automatic" techniques to free the artist's subconscious in a direct, spontaneous expression. Duchamp might seem to have had little influence on such a movement, but only if one completely ignores his contribution to the general climate of artistic freedom and experimentation in which it flourished.

However, there is little question that Duchamp's singular revolutionary work of the 1920s and 1930s anticipated the well-publicized styles of the 1950s and 1960s. One of these styles, Op Art, exploited the science of optics, teasing and fooling the eye in the manner of Duchamp's *Rotoreliefs*. Pop Art celebrates the peculiar beauty of commonplace objects like those used in Duchamp's readymades. Finally, there are such advanced experimenters as Robert Rauschenberg and Jasper Johns, artists so original that they belong to no movements. Still, as they freely admit, they find support in Duchamp's artistic philosophy, and inspiration in his works.

At home in his New York City apartment, Marcel Duchamp relaxes at one of his chessboards, this one with pieces designed by Max Ernst. "He was always more interested in taking risks in order to play a beautiful, artistic game," said chess grand master Edward Lasker, "than in being cautious and brutal in order to win."

Matta: *The Bachelors Twenty Years After*, 1943

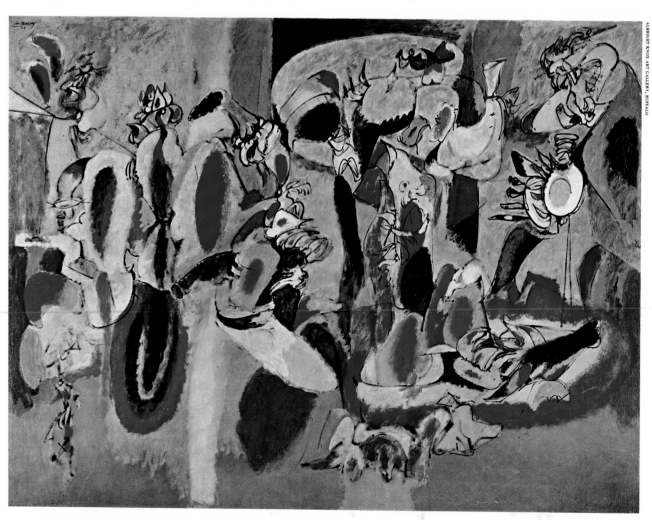

Arshile Gorky: *The Liver Is the Cock's Comb*, 1944

Jackson Pollock: *Number One*, 1948

Abstract Expressionism, launched in the 1940s by a group of artists in New York City, was the first school of American art to achieve international influence. It seized the imagination with large canvases, bold lines and vivid colors. Its origins, while intensely individual, lay partly in a rebellion against the intellectuality of Surrealism. A Chilean painter and friend of Duchamp's known as Matta began to go beyond Surrealism in such studies as the one at left above, in which he updated the master's perennial Bachelors *(page 89)*. Arshile Gorky, influenced by Matta, used Surrealist techniques but went still further: his work at left is a wild improvisation of free shapes with plumes of color.

It was with artists like Franz Kline and Jackson Pollock, however, that Abstract Expressionism reached its full power. Kline refined his style down to bold slashes of black paint, creating symbolic images evocative of Japanese calligraphy *(right)*. Pollock, breaking entirely with the traditional use of the brush and standard artists' pigments, dribbled and splattered automobile paints on his canvases to create an "art of raw sensations."

Franz Kline: *New York,* 1953

Even the rebellious pioneers of Action Painting found rebels to their cause. Partly as a reaction to the vivid emotionalism of Abstract Expressionism, the new school of Op Art rose to prominence in the 1960s, concentrating on meticulous draftsmanship and scientific effects. Like other schools, Op had its precedents in earlier experiments. For example, Duchamp's *Coeurs volants (below)*, created for a magazine cover in 1936, is a simple illustration of a well-known optical phenomenon. Its peculiar

Marcel Duchamp: *Coeurs volants*, 1936

pulsating effect is achieved by the juxtaposition of two strong primary colors; the red seems to advance while the blue appears to recede. The same principle, with a geometric twist, was used in 1963 by Victor de Vasarely in *Kalota (below)*. Not only does each form flutter within its square but each square seems to jiggle uneasily in relation to its neighbor. Works like these embody Op's unique characteristic; as art critic Emily Genauer once described it, "The viewer's eye is activated rather than just acted upon." This "activation" is unemotional; in the place of subject matter, the Op artist introduces sheer, eye-bulging sensation. Instead of the artist's personal brushstroke, the viewer finds forms shaped by the draftsman's straightedge. And in place of traditional, soft-toned oil pigments, Op offers a spectrum of brilliant new synthetic paints. Whether or not these precise and titillating images will become a part of art's permanent repertoire remains to be seen.

Victor de Vasarely: *Kalota*, 1963

Robert Rauschenberg: *Bed*, 1955

Robert Rauschenberg: *Monogram*, 1955-1959

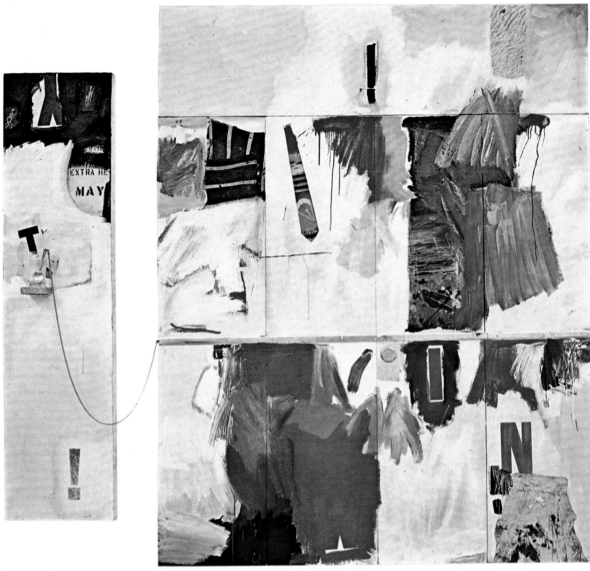

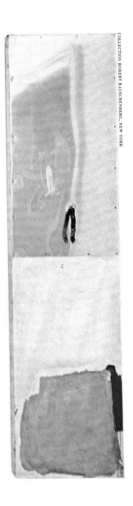

Robert Rauschenberg: *Trophy II (for Tini and Marcel Duchamp)*, 1960-1961

No single movement has been able to contain the varied styles of Robert Rauschenberg, who, like Duchamp, continually questions the very nature of art. "A painting is not art simply because it is made of oil and paint or because it is on canvas," he has said. Indeed, one day in 1955, when he was so broke he could not afford to buy a canvas, Rauschenberg stretched his bed quilt over a frame. "It looked strange without a pillow," he said, so he added one and then proceeded to dribble paint over it, naming the resulting creation *Bed (upper left)*.

Like Duchamp, Rauschenberg has been fascinated with everyday objects. He calls Duchamp's *Bicycle Wheel (slipcase)* "one of the most beautiful pieces of sculpture I've ever seen." He himself uses many similar things in works that he calls "combines" —artfully arranged collages of cast-off objects mixed with photographs as well as silk-screened and painted elements. His best-known combine is *Monogram (left)*, a painted platform on which stands a stuffed and carefully groomed Angora goat, with an old rubber tire around its belly and its face thickly "made up" with paint. His *Trophy II (above)*, a three-panel work dedicated to Duchamp and his wife, includes a hand-painted tie and a water-filled glass with a chained spoon in it.

179

Roy Lichtenstein: *Image Duplicator*, 1963

Is Pop Art a joke? Can an artist like James Rosenquist, who paints enormous canvases in the style of advertising billboards *(above)*, be taken seriously? Does Roy Lichtenstein, who uses both the technique and the imagery of the comic strip *(left)*, expect to be hung in a museum next to a Rembrandt? These are the very questions Pop Art itself asks. Rosenquist, who once painted billboards for a living, chose some well-known accoutrements of modern society for his 120-foot-long painting *F-111*, among them a hair dryer, a light bulb and an atomic mushroom cloud—all superimposed on a segmented rendering of a jet fighter plane. For his work *Marilyn*

James Rosenquist: *F-111*, 1965

(right), Andy Warhol chose just one famous American symbol, and for emphasis altered a photograph of her face; he added his own garish colors and used the silk-screen technique, giving it the effect of a movie ad.

Though, like other movements, Pop Art has its lighter side, it must be taken seriously because of the large number of talented artists it has attracted and the varied and inventive expressions they have given the style. Since the Surrealists had already explored the world of dreams, and the Abstract Expressionists had plumbed their own innermost emotions, the most compelling area left for the Pop Artists was the garish, transistorized, neon-lit world.

Andy Warhol: *Marilyn*, 1962

Jasper Johns: *Painted Bronze (Beer Cans)*, 1960

Like Rauschenberg and Duchamp, the American Jasper Johns is an individualist in the extreme. Working with conventional materials, he poses unconventional questions about the nature of reality and art. His work at left appears to consist of two actual ale cans on a base, but in reality it is a bronze sculpture with lettering. Nor is his *Map (right)* a real map but a painting in which Johns used a familiar shape as a framework for a play of colors. Below, Johns again plays with color, in vivid fields and spectral arcs "brushed" on with rulers, in perhaps the most adventuresome work of the mid-1960s. Here, his subject is painting itself and its essential ingredients: color, line, canvas, paint; a broom, perhaps to represent the artist's brush; and even two impressions of the artist's own hand.

Jasper Johns: *Map*, 1961

Jasper Johns: *Untitled Painting*, 1965

Chronology: Artists of Duchamp's Era

FRANCE
PAUL CÉZANNE 1839-1906
ODILON REDON 1840-1916
AUGUSTE RODIN 1840-1917
HENRI ROUSSEAU 1844-1910
PAUL GAUGUIN 1848-1903
GEORGES SEURAT 1859-1891
HENRI TOULOUSE-LAUTREC 1864-1901
EDOUARD VUILLARD 1868-1940
HENRI MATISSE 1869-1954
GEORGES ROUAULT 1871-1958
JACQUES VILLON 1875-1963
RAYMOND DUCHAMP-VILLON 1876-1918
FRANCIS PICABIA 1879-1953
ANDRE DERAIN 1880-1954
ALBERT GLEIZES 1881-1953
FERNAND LÉGER 1881-1955
GEORGES BRAQUE 1882-1963
JEAN METZINGER 1883-1956
ROGER DE LA FRESNAYE 1885-1925
ROBERT DELAUNAY 1885-1941
JEAN ARP 1887-1966
MARCEL DUCHAMP 1887-1968
JACQUES LIPCHITZ 1891-1973
YVES TANGUY 1900-1955
JEAN DUBUFFET 1901-
ROBERTO MATTA ECHAURREN 1912-

GERMANY
LOVIS CORINTH 1858-1925
EMIL NOLDE 1867-1956
MAX BECKMANN 1884-1950
KURT SCHWITTERS 1887-1948
HANS RICHTER 1888-1976
MAX ERNST 1891-1976
RICHARD HUELSENBECK 1892-
HANS HARTUNG 1904-

HOLLAND
VINCENT VAN GOGH 1853-1890
PIET MONDRIAN 1872-1944
THEO VAN DOESBERG 1883-1931

BELGIUM
PAUL DELVAUX 1897-
RENÉ MAGRITTE 1898-1967

EASTERN EUROPE
FRANK KUPKA (CZECH) 1871-1957
CONSTANTIN BRANCUSI (ROMANIAN) 1876-1957
MARCEL JANCO (ROMANIAN) 1895-
VICTOR DE VASARELY (HUNGARIAN) 1908-

RUSSIA
WASSILY KANDINSKY 1866-1944
CASIMIR MALEVICH 1878-1935
ANTOINE PEVSNER 1886-1962
ALEXANDER ARCHIPENKO 1887-1964
MARC CHAGALL 1887-
NAUM GABO 1890-1966

SCANDINAVIA
EDVARD MUNCH 1863-1944
VIKING EGGELING 1880-1925

SPAIN
PABLO PICASSO 1881-1973
JUAN GRIS 1887-1927
JOAN MIRÓ 1893-
SALVADOR DALI 1904-

ITALY
GIACOMO BALLA 1871-1958
CARLO CARRÀ 1881-1966
UMBERTO BOCCIONI 1882-1916
GINO SEVERINI 1883-1966
AMEDEO MODIGLIANI 1884-1920
GIORGIO DE CHIRICO 1888-

SWITZERLAND
JEAN CROTTI 1878-1958
PAUL KLEE 1879-1940
ALBERTO GIACOMETTI 1901-1966
MERET OPPENHEIM 1913-
JEAN TINGUELY 1925-

UNITED STATES
MAURICE PRENDERGAST 1859-1924
JOHN MARIN 1870-1953
JOSEPH STELLA 1877-1946
ARTHUR DOVE 1880-1946
WALT KUHN 1880-1949
HANS HOFMANN 1880-1966
GEORGE BELLOWS 1882-1925
EDWARD HOPPER 1882-1967
CHARLES DEMUTH 1883-1935
CHARLES SHEELER 1883-1965
GEORGIA O'KEEFFE 1887-
MAN RAY 1890-1976
MARK TOBEY 1890-1976
ALEXANDER CALDER 1898-
BEN SHAHN 1898-1969
JOSEPH CORNELL 1903-1972
MARK ROTHKO 1903-1970
ARSHILE GORKY 1904-1948
WILLEM DE KOONING 1904-
FRANZ KLINE 1910-1962
JACKSON POLLOCK 1912-1956
ROBERT MOTHERWELL 1915-
ROY LICHTENSTEIN 1923-
LARRY RIVERS 1923-
ROBERT RAUSCHENBERG 1925-
ROBERT INDIANA 1928-
CLAES OLDENBURG 1929-
JASPER JOHNS 1930-
ANDY WARHOL 1930-
RONALD B. KITAJ 1932-
JAMES ROSENQUIST 1933-
JIM DINE 1935-

ENGLAND
AUGUSTUS JOHN 1879-1961
JACOB EPSTEIN 1880-1959
BEN NICHOLSON 1894-
HENRY MOORE 1898-
FRANCIS BACON 1910-

Duchamp's predecessors and contemporaries are grouped here in chronological order according to country. The bands correspond to the life-spans of the artists.

Bibliography   *Available in paperback

MARCEL DUCHAMP

Hamilton, Richard, *The Bride Stripped Bare by Her Bachelors, Even (a typographic version of Marcel Duchamp's Green Box)*. Translated by George Heard Hamilton. Wittenborn, 1960.

Lebel, Robert, *Marcel Duchamp*. Translated by George Heard Hamilton. Grove, 1959.

*Sanouillet, Michel (editor), *Marchand du Sel*. Le Terrain Vague, 1958.

View. Marcel Duchamp Number, Series V, No. 1. 1945.

MARCEL DUCHAMP CATALOGUES

d'Harnoncourt, Anne and Kynaston McShine, *Marcel Duchamp*. Museum of Modern Art and Philadelphia Museum of Art, 1973.

Hopps, Walter, Ulf Linde and Arturo Schwarz, *Marcel Duchamp: Ready-Mades, etc. (1913-1964)*. Galleria Schwarz, 1964.

*Not Seen and/or Less Seen of/by Marcel Duchamp/Rrose Sélavy: Mary Sisler Collection. Cordier & Ekstrom, 1965.

*Pasadena Art Museum, *by or of Marcel Duchamp or Rrose Sélavy*, 1963.

Schwarz, Arturo, *The Complete Works of Marcel Duchamp*. Abrams, 1970.

*Tate Gallery Exhibition. *The almost complete works of Marcel Duchamp*. Arts Council of Great Britain, 1966.

HISTORY OF ART: PERIODS AND STYLES

*Amaya, Mario, *Pop Art . . . and After*. Viking, 1972.

Barr, Alfred H., Jr. (editor), *Fantastic Art, Dada, Surrealism*. Museum of Modern Art, 1970.

Masters of Modern Art. The Museum of Modern Art, 1958.

*Breton, André, *What Is Surrealism?* Translated by David Gascoyne. Haskell, 1973.

Surrealism and Painting. Translated by Samuel Taylor. Harper & Row, 1973.

Brown, Milton W., *The Story of the Armory Show*. New York Graphic Society, 1963.

Delevoy, Robert L., *Dimensions of the 20th Century: 1900-1945*. Translated by Stuart Gilbert. Skira, 1965.

Dorival, Bernard, *The School of Paris in the Musée d'Art Moderne*. Translated by Cornelia Brookfield and Ellen Hart. Abrams, 1962.

Dorra, Henri, *Years of Ferment: The Birth of Twentieth Century Art 1886-1914*. University of California Art Council, 1965.

*Fowlie, Wallace, *Age of Surrealism*. Peter Smith, 1960.

Gascoyne, David, *Short Survey of Surrealism*. R. Cobden-Sanderson Ltd., 1935.

Geldzahler, Henry, *American Painting in the Twentieth Century*. The Metropolitan Museum of Art, 1965.

Habasque, Guy, *Cubism*. Translated by Stuart Gilbert, Skira, 1959.

*Haftmann, Werner, *Painting in the Twentieth Century* (2 Vols.). Praeger, 1965.

Janis, Sidney, *Abstract & Surrealist Art in America*. Arno.

Jean, Marcel, with Arpad Mezei, *History of Surrealist Painting*. Translated by Simon Watson Taylor. Grove, 1960.

Matthews, J. H., *Introduction to Surrealism*. Pennsylvania State University Press, 1965.

Motherwell, Robert (editor), *Dada Painters and Poets: An Anthology*. Wittenborn & Schultz, 1951.

Nadeau, Maurice, *The History of Surrealism*. Translated by Richard Howard. Macmillan, 1965.

*Raymond, Marcel, *From Baudelaire to Surrealism*. Wittenborn & Schultz, 1950.

Raynal, Maurice, *Modern Painting*. Translated by Stuart Gilbert. Skira, 1960.

Read, Herbert (editor), *Surrealism*. Praeger, 1972.

Concise History of Modern Painting. Praeger, 1975.

Richter, Hans, *Dada: Art and Anti-Art*. McGraw-Hill, 1966.

Rosenblum, Robert, *Cubism and Twentieth-Century Art*. Abrams, 1976.

Rublowsky, John, with photography by Kenneth Heyman, *Pop Art*. Basic Books, 1965.

*Shattuck, Roger, *The Banquet Years: The Arts in France, 1885-1918*. Random House, 1968.

*Taylor, Joshua C., *Futurism*. Museum of Modern Art, 1961.

Verkauf, Willy (editor), and others, *Dada: Monograph of a Movement*. St. Martin, 1976.

Waldberg, Patrick, *Surrealism*. Translated by Stuart Gilbert. Skira, 1962.

OTHER ARTISTS

Dali, Salvador, *Diary of a Genius*. Translated by Richard Howard. Doubleday, 1965.

Secret Life of Salvador Dali. Translated by Haakon M. Chevalier. Dial, 1961.

Descharnes, Robert, *The World of Salvador Dali*. Translated by Albert Field and Haakon M. Chevalier. Harper & Row, 1962.

Dupin, Jacques, *Miró*. Translated by Norbert Guterman. Abrams, 1962.

*Ernst, Max, *Beyond Painting, and Other Writings by the Artist and His Friends*. Wittenborn & Schultz, 1948.

Greenberg, Clement, *Joan Miró*. Arno.

Hahn, Otto (editor), *Masson*. Translated by Robert Erich Wolf. Abrams, 1965.

Klee, Felix (editor), *The Diaries of Paul Klee: 1898-1918*. University of California Press, 1964.

Paul Klee. Translated by Richard and Clara Winston. George Braziller, 1962.

Lassaigne, Jacques, *Miró*. Skira, 1963.

Schwabacher, Ethel K., *Arshile Gorky*. The Whitney Museum of American Art, 1957.

Soby, James Thrall (editor), *arp*. Museum of Modern Art, 1958.

After Picasso. Dodd, Mead, 1935.

Giorgio de Chirico. Museum of Modern Art, 1955.

Salvador Dali. Museum of Modern Art, 1946.

Joan Miró. Museum of Modern Art, 1959.

Sweeney, James Johnson, "Joan Miró: Comment and Interview," *Partisan Review*, February 1948.

Waldberg, Patrick, *Max Ernst*. Edited by Jean-Jacques Pauvert. Société des Editions, 1958.

OTHER ARTISTS' CATALOGUES

*Gallery of Modern Art Exhibition, *Salvador Dali*. Foundation for Modern Art, 1965.

*Hunter, Sam (editor), *Max Ernst: Sculpture and Recent Painting*. Jewish Museum, 1966.

Jackson Pollock. Museum of Modern Art, 1956.

*Lieberman, William S. (editor), *Max Ernst*. Museum of Modern Art, 1961.

Marlborough-Gerson Gallery Exhibition, *Kurt Schwitters*. Marlborough Fine Art Ltd., 1965.

*Penrose, Roland, *Joan Miró*. Marlborough-Gerson Gallery Exhibition. Marlborough Fine Art Ltd., 1966.

*Rubin, William, *Matta*. Museum of Modern Art, 1957.

*Seitz, William C., *Arshile Gorky: Paintings, Drawings, Studies*. Museum of Modern Art, 1962.

The Art of Assemblage. Museum of Modern Art, 1961.

Selz, Peter (editor), *Alberto Giacometti*. Museum of Modern Art, 1965.

*Soby, James Thrall, *René Magritte*. Museum of Modern Art, 1965.

Yves Tanguy. Museum of Modern Art, 1956.

*Solomon, Alan R., *Robert Rauschenberg*. Jewish Museum, 1963.

*Solomon, Alan R. and John Cage (editors), *Jasper Johns*. Jewish Museum, 1964.

Sweeney, James Johnson, *Marc Chagall*. Museum of Modern Art, 1946.

LITERATURE

*Breton, André, *Nadja*. Translated by Richard Howard. Peter Smith, 1960.

Ducasse, Isadore (pen name Comte de Lautréamont), *Les Chants de Maldoror*. Skira, 1934.

*Jarry, Alfred, *Ubu Roi*. Translated by Barbara Wright. New Directions, 1961.

*Rimbaud, Arthur, *Illuminations and Other Prose Poems*. Translated by Louise Varèse. New Directions, 1957.

Steegmuller, Francis, *Apollinaire: Poet among the Painters*. Farrar, Straus and Giroux, 1963.

Wilson, Edmund, *Axel's Castle: A Study in the Imaginative Literature of 1870-1930*. Scribner, 1931.

GENERAL

*Apollinaire, Guillaume, *The Cubist Painters: Aesthetic Meditations 1913*. Translated by Lionel Abel. Wittenborn, 1962.

Courthion, Pierre, *Paris in Our Time*. Skira, 1957.

Guggenheim, Peggy, *Confessions of an Art Addict*. Macmillan, 1960.

Josephson, Matthew, *Life among the Surrealists*. Holt, Rinehart and Winston, 1962.

*Picabia, Francis, *391*. Series of periodicals collected and edited by Michel Sanouillet. Le Terrain Vague, 1960.

Tomkins, Calvin, *The Bride and the Bachelors: The Heretical Courtship in Modern Art*. Viking, 1968.

Acknowledgments

For their help in the production of this book the editors wish to acknowledge the following people: Mrs. George Acheson, New York; Jean Adhémar, Conservateur en Chef du Cabinet des Estampes de la Bibliothèque Nationale, Paris; Kay Bearman, Leo Castelli and David Whitney, Leo Castelli Gallery, New York; André Breton, Paris; Louis Carré, Paris; Mr. and Mrs. Marcel Duchamp, New York; Arne Ekstrom, Cordier & Ekstrom, Inc., New York; Ellen Franklin and Henry Geldzahler, The Metropolitan Museum of Art; Rose Fried Gallery, New York; Henry Gardner, Hobart Lyle Williams and Alfred J. Wyatt, Philadelphia Museum of Art; Marie Moelle de Grandy, Musée National d'Art Moderne, Paris; Peggy Guggenheim, Venice; Henry Street Settlement, New York; Philippe Halsman, New York; Joseph H. Hirshhorn Foundation, New York; Dr. Charles Hulbeck, New York; Georges Hugnet, Paris; Robert J. Jaczko, Wadsworth Atheneum, Hartford, Connecticut; Sidney Janis Gallery, New York; Abram Lerner, Curator, Joseph H. Hirshhorn Collection, New York; Julien Levy, Paris; René Magritte, Brussels; Signore and Signora Gianni Mattioli, Milan; Garnett McCoy, Archives of American Art, Detroit; E.L.T. Mesens, London; Pearl Moeller and Richard Tooke, The Museum of Modern Art, New York; Fredric Mueller, New York; Munson-Williams-Proctor Institute, Utica; Mr. and Mrs. Eliot Noyes, Connecticut; Roland Penrose, London; Yves Poupard-Lieussou, Vice-President of the Dada Association, Paris; Hans Richter, Ascona, Switzerland; Man Ray, Paris; Arturo Schwarz, Galleria Schwarz, Milan; Mrs. Mary Sisler, New York; Henry Torczyner, New York; Yale University Art Gallery, Société Anonyme, New Haven.

Picture Credits

The sources for the illustrations in this book appear below. Credits for pictures from left to right are separated by semicolons, from top to bottom by dashes.

SLIPCASE:
Lee Boltin.

END PAPERS:
Mark Kauffman.

CHAPTER 1: 6—Marvin P. Lazarus. 10, 11—Eddy Van der Veen. 12—Mary Sisler Collection photo by Geoffrey Clements. 13—Eddy Van der Veen. 14—Derek Bayes. 15—Lee Boltin. 17—Lee Boltin. 18—Lee Boltin; Eddy Van der Veen (2). 19—Lee Boltin. 20 through 25—Lee Boltin except 21 right: Archives of American Art. 26—Laurent Sully from Rapho Guillumette; Emmett Bright—Lee Boltin. 27—Lee Boltin.

CHAPTER 2: 28, 29—Lee Boltin. 32—From Alfred Jarry, *Ubu Roi*, © 1961 by New Directions. Reprinted by permission of the publisher, New Directions Publishing Corporation—Alfred J. Wyatt. 34—Museum of Modern Art photos. 36—Attilio Bacci. 38—Cordier & Ekstrom, Inc. photo by Geoffrey Clements. 39—Attilio Bacci. 40, 41—Walt Kuhn Papers, Archives of American Art—inset: Lee Boltin. 42, 43—Top: Lee Boltin. Center: Lee Boltin (2); Museum of Modern Art photo. Bottom: Museum of Modern Art photo. 44, 45—Lee Boltin. 46, 47—Frank Lerner; Baltimore Museum of Art photo—Robert S. Crandall. 48, 49—Left: Lee Boltin (2). Right: Henry Street Settlement photo—Cliché des Musées Nationaux. 50, 51—Henry Street Settlement photo by Lee Boltin. 52, 53—Left: Robert S. Crandall. Right: Henry Street Settlement photo—Lee Boltin.

CHAPTER 3: 54—Derek Bayes. 56—Museum of Modern Art photos. 58—Charles Phillips—Museum of Modern Art photo. 59—Museum of Modern Art photo—Eddy Van der Veen. 61—Lee Boltin. 66—© Ringier-Bilderdienst, Zurich. 67—© J. H. Bruell, Zurich. 68, 69—Museum of Modern Art photo; Hermann Vogel (2)—Candid Lang. 70—André Villers. 71—Eric Schaal—Art Institute of Chicago photo. 72—Emmett Bright. 73—Attilio Bacci; Lee Boltin—Emmett Bright. 74—Niedersachsische Landesgalerie, Hanover—Marlborough-Gerson Gallery Inc. photo; Heinz Zinram.

CHAPTER 4: 76—Lee Boltin. 78—Eddy Van der Veen. 79—Collection Man Ray, Paris. 80—Attilio Bacci. 81—Mary Sisler Collection photo by Geoffrey Clements. 83—Lee Boltin. 84—Museum of Modern Art photo—Lee Boltin. 85, 86, 87—Lee Boltin except 85 top right: Alfred J. Wyatt. 88 through 91—Alfred J. Wyatt except 90 top: Collection Man Ray, Paris. 92, 93—Top: Alfred J. Wyatt.

CHAPTER 5: 94, 96—Collection Man Ray, Paris. 98—Lee Boltin. 101—Museum of Modern Art photo by Soichi Sunami. 102—Museum of Modern Art photo. 103, 105—Museum of Modern Art photos by Soichi Sunami. 106—Eddy Van der Veen. 109—Photo courtesy Modern Museum of Stockholm, André Breton Collection. 110—Museum of Modern Art photo. 111—Left: Collection Man Ray, Paris. 112—Top: Art Institute of Chicago photo. 113, 114—Lee Boltin. 115—© Museum of Modern Art; Lee Boltin—Aldo Durazzi. 116—Derek Bayes. 117—© Museum of Modern Art. 118, 119—Lee Boltin except center bottom: © Museum of Modern Art. 120—Emmett Bright—Henry Groskinsky. 121—Henry Groskinsky.

CHAPTER 6: 122—© Museum of Modern Art. 124—© Philippe Halsman. 125—Photo courtesy The Gallery of Modern Art including the Huntington Hartford Collection. 128—Photos courtesy Owen Cheatham Foundation, New York. 132—Museum of Modern Art photo. 134—Photo courtesy Collection Gerald Cramer, Geneva—photo courtesy Boris Kochno from *Le Ballet* published by Editions du Chêne. 135—Lisa Larsen. 136, 137, 138—© Philippe Halsman. 139—Robert Descharnes. 140—Lee Boltin. 141—Robert Descharnes. 142—Fernand Bourges—Robert Descharnes. 143—© Rijksmuseum, Amsterdam—Emmett Bright. 144, 145—© Museum of Modern Art; Lee Boltin (3). 146, 147—Lee Boltin.

CHAPTER 7: 149—Attilio Bacci. 150 through 156—Museum of Modern Art photos by Soichi Sunami except 156 bottom: Denise Bellon from Images et Textes, Paris. 159—United Press International. 160—Alan Clifton—Denise Bellon from Images et Textes. 161—United Press International—Denise Bellon from Images et Textes. 162, 163—Rose Fried Gallery photo by John D. Schiff; Bill Ray—Denise Bellon from Images et Textes; Jean Marquis.

CHAPTER 8: 164—Ken Heyman. 165—Ben Martin. 166—Mary Sisler Collection photo by Barney Burstein. 167—Philadelphia Museum of Art: Gift of the Cassandra Foundation. 169—Bottom: Museum of Modern Art photo. 170—Richard Hamilton. 173—Mark Kauffman. 174, 175—Top: Lee Boltin (2). Bottom: Frank Lerner (2). 176—Attilio Bacci. 177—Savage Studios, St. Louis. 178, 179—Lee Boltin; Hans Hammarskiöld/Tio, Stockholm; Leo Castelli Gallery photo by Eric Pollitzer. 180, 181—Leo Castelli Gallery photo by Eric Pollitzer—Herbert Orth; Robert S. Crandall. 182, 183—Top: Leo Castelli Gallery photos by Rudolph Burckhardt (2)—Leo Castelli Gallery photo by Eric Pollitzer. 184—Chart by George V. Kelvin.

Index